How to Pass

FCE

First Certificate in English

Exam practice in
Listening and
Speaking

PAPERS FOUR & FIVE

Amber

Catherine Wrangham-Briggs

Contents

This book tells you what to expect in the Listening and Speaking papers of the new (1996) Cambridge First Certificate Examination and helps you understand:
- how these two papers are organised
- what level of skill is expected
- what you are likely to find in them
- how you can prepare yourself for the different kinds of tasks set.

You will find the step-by-step guidance in this book easy to follow and useful, especially if you are preparing for the exam on your own. You can also use the book if you are learning to communicate in English but have little opportunity to hear natural English or to have frequent conversations in English. The exercises, explanations and advice in this book will all help to improve your fluency and understanding.

The first part of the book is on the Listening Paper and there is a complete Trial Exam Paper at the end of it. The second part of the book is about the Speaking Paper and gives Practice Exercises with explanations and advice throughout. You can read more about the Speaking Paper on page 2.

PAPER 4: LISTENING

The Listening Paper has 4 parts. There are 30 questions altogether and it takes about 40 minutes. The Listening part of this book is also divided into 4 parts, to match the examination parts. This is a brief description of the exam itself:

You listen to a tape recording and the tasks are presented on paper. You write on the question paper while you are listening and you are given time at the end of the test to transfer your answers to a special answer sheet. (On page 78 there is a special answer sheet which you can use when you do the Trial Paper).

Part 1
Questions 1 - 8: eight spoken texts about 30 seconds long each, with one Multiple Choice question for each.

Part 2
Questions 9 - 18: one spoken text about 3 minutes long, with 10 boxes to complete with one or more words.

Part 3
Questions 19 - 23: five related spoken texts about 30 seconds long each, with five answers to choose from a list of six possibilities. The task is to match speaker to text.

Part 4
Questions 24 - 30: one spoken text about 3 minutes long, with 7 questions. These questions are either Multiple Choice or True/False or 'Who said what?'

Using the book
Each part of the book follows a pattern. This is how the parts are arranged:

Looking at Part ...
This gives you detailed information about what you have to do in this part of the exam.

What's Being Tested
This tells you what the examiner will be looking out for particularly.

Doing the Exam
Here you will find hints and advice on how to approach this particular part of the exam.

Practice Exercises
These are graded. You will start with some exercises which are shorter and easier than those in the exam, and gradually build up to the more difficult ones in the next section.

Exam Exercises

These are exercises which are the same level of difficulty and length as the ones in the exam. The spoken texts for the Practice Exercises and the Exam Exercises are not repeated on the accompanying tape. So when you want to hear them a second time, just rewind your tape to the right place to listen again.

Self Assessment

Thinking carefully about your own strengths, weaknesses and the progress you are making is a big part of learning, so it is very important to take your time over answering the questions that you find in this section.

Trial Paper

Finally, there is a complete Trial Paper containing all 4 parts, which you can try under exam conditions. This means that you can listen straight through on the tape recorder without rewinding any part of it. All the spoken texts for the Trial Paper are repeated with the right pauses already put in (except for five minutes right at the end for transferring your answers onto the special answer sheet), just as it will be in the exam, so once you have started the tape there is no need to touch it until the end.

Answers, Notes and Tapescript

Detailed explanations and language help are given under this heading, as well as the tapescript for all the spoken texts in the exercises, to help you see why you went wrong if you did, and to make sure you make fewer mistakes next time.

Marks

Every question in the Listening Paper carries one mark. Furthermore, all five papers in the First Certificate carry equal weight, even though the number of questions is not the same. That is, each of the 5 papers carries 20% of the total marks. In order to pass the First Certificate, you need to reach an overall mark of about 60% across the 5 papers. This means that although in theory you could fail one of the papers and still pass First Certificate, you would have to do extraordinarily well in all the others to pass. So it is certainly worth aiming for 60% or above in each of the papers.

The Cassette

Where you see this symbol in the book, it means the text is on the cassette. For all the Practice Exercises and the Exam Exercises in Chapters 2-5, the text is only spoken once. You will therefore have to rewind the cassette to listen again. For the Trial Paper, the texts are spoken twice, as in the exam.

Side 1: Part 1 Practice Exercise 1– Part 4 Practice Exercise 5.
Side 2: Part 4 Practice Exercise 6– end.

PAPER 5: SPEAKING

Like the Listening Paper, the Speaking Paper has 4 parts. It takes about fifteen minutes altogether. There will normally be two Examiners in the room. One of these is called the Interlocutor. The interlocutor is the person who joins in some of the conversations with you and will give you instructions. The other Examiner is called the Assessor. The assessor takes no part in the conversations with you, the candidate, but he or she will be listening to you and marking your performance. After the exam is over and you have left the room, the assessor will discuss your overall performance with the interlocutor and decide what marks to give you.

This is how the exam is organised:

Part 1

Interview between an interlocutor and one candidate. Three minutes.

Part 2

Two candidates talking separately about a pair of related photographs. Four minutes.

Part 3

Discussion between 2 candidates to solve a problem or come to a decision. Three minutes.

Part 4

Discussion between two candidates and an interlocutor about a subject related to the theme in Part 3. Four minutes.

The pattern of the book

This part of the book is arranged in a similar way to the Listening part except that there are no Exam Exercises or timed Trial Paper here. Because it is a Speaking Paper, this would be impossible to arrange without having an assessor there with you to talk to. However, the Practice Exercises are of the same standard, content and length as the ones you will find in the exam. You will find therefore that they will give you a clear idea of what to expect. You will also get a clear idea of what is expected of you because the *Useful Language* sections are extremely full and detailed. They give you the maximum possible advice about the kinds of things you should say in the Speaking Paper, with suggestions of how to express and organise them. As before, each part also has Self Assessment questions to remind you of how you are doing.

Marks

Marks are given for your ability to use your spoken language skills effectively. There are a number of important points to bear in mind about how candidates are assessed in the Speaking Paper:

- You must speak enough for the assessor to be able to judge your ability fairly.
- Remember that it is up to the candidates to keep the conversations going as much as possible and your ability to do this carries marks.
- It is not a test of listening, so if you don't understand something or feel you have been misunderstood, it is important to ask the other speaker to explain or give an explanation yourself. In fact your ability to sort out this kind of misunderstanding is something the examiner will be assessing.
- It is not absolutely essential to complete the task you are given. You must work towards it but if it isn't finished within the time, this doesn't matter.

Information about the passmark of the 5 papers in the exam is on page 2.

LOOKING AT PART 1

Questions 1 - 8 form Part 1 of the Listening Paper. You will find the questions on the tape as well as on the paper and you will hear each spoken text twice. Each of the 8 spoken texts is a separate monologue (that is, one person speaking) or conversation (two people speaking). Each one is about 30 seconds long. The spoken texts may be complete in themselves, like a weather forecast or news item, or you may get part of a longer piece, such as part of a job interview or a conversation on a bus.

ANSWERING THE QUESTIONS

Each of the 8 questions gives you some information about the context or situation that you will hear. On the the next line there will be a question, followed by three possible answers, A, B and C. Only one is correct. Your job is to listen to the text, decide which is the right answer and write A, B or C in the empty box on the right. This is how it is set out:

1 Listen to this girl arguing on the phone with her boyfriend.
What is she angry about?

   A He borrowed her car without asking.
   B He left her car in a carpark.
   C He forgot to meet her at six o'clock.

                                                              `1`

Filling in the answer sheet
At the end of the test, you will be given time to transfer your answers to the special answer sheet (see page 78). Be very careful to put the right answer by the right number.

WHAT'S BEING TESTED

These multiple choice questions often ask you about what happened or other facts. But they may also ask you about different things. As well as needing to understand the general idea or the main points being made, you may also find questions about any of these:

- the purpose of the communication
- where it's taking place
- who the people are in relation to each other
- how they feel
- the speaker's opinion or intention.

So it's not just a matter of the words that the speakers use. It's also important to try and think yourself into what you are hearing, even though it's very short. Occasionally there may be some background sounds to help you, but usually there won't be.

PRACTICE EXERCISES

To help you think about some of the points mentioned above, listen to the short items in the first three Practice Exercises and answer the questions about them. Remember that this is not how the questions are put in the exam (see example above for the exam format) – the Practice Exercises in this book are to help you build up your listening techniques first, before you try the Exam Exercises. The answers, notes and tapescripts are on pages 52-55.

Saying who the speakers are and where they are

Llisten to five different spoken texts and in each case say who is talking, where they are and how you know the answers. Listen to each one twice before moving on to the next one.

PRACTICE EXERCISE 1

1 Who?   Where?   How do you know?
2 Who?   Where?   How do you know?
3 Who?   Where?   How do you know?
4 Who?   Where?   How do you know?
5 Who?   Where?   How do you know?

Now check your answers on page 52.

Listening for the speaker's purpose

PRACTICE EXERCISE 2

In Practice Exercise 2, each of the five items you will hear has a different purpose. Read the questions carefully, as you would read exam questions. Then listen to the tape and write the correct speaker number in the space provided. Then listen again and answer questions a) and b). Then go on to the next one. Before you do the activity, read this note.

Note: You will see in the answers that some keywords are underlined. However, as I mentioned earlier, it isn't simply a matter of listening out for individual words and their meaning. It is sensible to think about words **in their context**. Here are some examples.

In English, some words are often found with certain other words, like *a trail of smoke*, or *highly qualified*.

Also words in context may have a positive or negative feeling about them: for example, if a speaker starts with the words: *It's true that*... it suggests that the second part of the sentence may begin with *but*... .

In other cases, the choice of words can put an image into the listener's mind. For example the words *Shall we go down in the lift* would be very likely to put a particular idea into your mind. Even if you can't say for sure how you know the answer, it is always a good idea to try and imagine what is happening while you are listening. Have a picture in your mind of the speakers, where they might be, etc. and imagine in as much detail as possible everything that you hear.

Listen to the first two spoken texts in Practice Exercise 2. Make sure you listen to them twice. Decide which speaker is expressing an opinion and which is receiving directions, then listen again and answer a) and b) This exercise is also good practice for noticing and remembering which spoken text you are listening to. This is very important in the First Certificate Listening Exam.

Speaker no. _____ is expressing an opinion.
  a) What about?   b) How do you know?

Speaker no _____ is receiving directions.
  a) To where?   b) How do you know?

Now check your answers on page 53.

This time there are three spoken texts for you to sort out. Again, listen to them each twice, decide which speaker is apologising, which is reporting and which is describing, and then answer the questions.

Speaker no. _____ is apologising.
  a) Apologising for what?   b) How do you know?

Speaker no. _____ is reporting.
  a) Reporting on what?   b) How do you know?

Speaker no. _____ is describing.
  a) Describing what?   b) How do you know?

Now check your answers on page 53.

**PRACTICE
EXERCISE 3**

Understanding the message

For the six short items in Practice Exercise 3, you will find a clue sentence giving the context, as it is in the exam. For example: **1** Two friends have met in town . This time though, you must choose from Yes/No/Maybe for each question. In Practice Exercise 4 you will get some practice in doing multiple choice questions of the sort in the exam. For now, this question tests to see whether you have understood an important point in the communication.

1 Two friends have met in town. Is the first speaker buying train tickets?	Yes No Maybe
2 A man is being interviewed by a journalist. Is he looking forward to the new road?	Yes No Maybe
3 A doctor is talking to a patient in hospital. Has the patient got an infection?	Yes No Maybe
4 A customer has brought some goods back to a shop. Does the shop assistant agree to exchange the goods?	Yes No Maybe
5 The local news is on television. Does the Inspector believe handguns should be allowed in shooting clubs?	Yes No Maybe

Now check your answers on page 54.

**PRACTICE
EXERCISE 4**

In this exercise you have a chance to try some multiple choice questions like the ones in the exam. You're going to try two different ways of approaching these to see if one suits you better than the other. In the first three questions, look carefully at the clue sentence and think about the information it tells you – for instance, it may tell you who is talking, or where they are or what they are talking about. Then read the question. This will help you to think about what you are going to hear. Normally you would probably then read the three different possibilities (A, B and C) before listening. Sometimes, though, people find they get confused when they look at these. So, for the first three questions, try following these steps:

i)   Cover A, B and C with a piece of paper.
ii) Look at the clue sentence and the question.
iii) Listen to the spoken text *without looking at the choices A, B and C.*
iv) Make a note of what you think the answer might be.
v)   *Then* look at A, B and C and make your choice.
vi) Listen to the text a second time before your final decision.

(In the exam you will hear the choices A, B and C on the tape, so you can't do it quite like this, but this is still a useful exercise to try at this stage because it helps you to listen carefully.) For numbers 4 - 6, we'll do it by looking at A, B and C first, before any listening.

Now do Numbers 1 - 3 following the instructions above. Remember, start by covering A, B and C of Question 1.

1 A friend is giving you a recipe.   (*Clue sentence*)
What is he making?   (*Question*)

A brown bread
B bacon sandwiches
C omelette

	1

2 Listen to a woman explaining something.
  What is her problem?

A She may need reading glasses.
B She gets tired and unsteady.
C She's afraid of the dark.

☐ 2

3 Listen to this weather forecast.
  What will the weather be like by the sea?

A sunny
B dry and cold
C cold and wet

☐ 3

Now check the answers on page 54 to see which ones were correct, and decide if you liked this way of doing it.

For the next three questions, read the clue sentence and the question and also study A, B and C. Then listen to the spoken text twice and make your choice.

4 You hear this announcement on television.
  What happened?

A The man dropped the cheque and the police found it later.
B The man stole the cheque and tried to cash it at a bank.
C The man dropped the cheque and then someone stole it.

☐ 4

5 Listen to this person talking to a group of people.
  Who is talking to who?

A A music teacher is talking to his singing students.
B A bus driver is talking to his passengers.
C Someone is trying to take a photograph.

☐ 5

6 Kevin wants to speak to Jim on the phone.
  What has happened?

A Lindy thinks Kevin has called the wrong number.
B Lindy is sorry she's made a mistake about Jim Banks.
C Kevin thinks Lindy sounds mysterious.

☐ 6

Check your answers on page 54. Which approach did you find easier?

DOING THE EXAM

Here are some hints to help you with Part 1 of the Listening Paper.

Try to
- imagine the people, place and actions
- use the context (clue sentence) to help you understand the message
- open your mind and don't get fixed onto one thought – you need to be flexible in your approach
- keep listening, even if there is a word you don't understand
- choose an approach which best suits you, e.g. you may not want to think about A,B and C until you have heard the spoken text once.

Try not to panic before the test: - do some deep breathing exercises if you feel anxious
                                      - listen to something in English you know you can understand.

Try not to worry about understanding every word – the question may be an easy one which only demands that you understand the topic or location, or general purpose.

EXAM EXERCISES

The following two exercises are similar to those you will find in the exam. I am going to ask you to do one extra thing, though. When you have answered all the questions, go back to each question and write the words *very certain*, *fairly certain* or *not certain*, to indicate how sure of your answer you are. If you have a lucky guess in the exam, then that can be all right, but you should aim now to be as certain as possible. You will find this task in all the Exam Exercises in this book.

EXAM EXERCISE 1 You will hear 8 short spoken texts – each about 30 seconds long. Decide for each one whether A, B or C is the right answer. *Listen to each spoken text twice before you go on to the next one.*

1 Two friends are in a clothes shop.
Why does one of them want some new clothes?

A because she's going to a wedding
B because she's getting married
C because she's worried about what the guests might think

	1

2 Listen to this description.
What is being described?

A an African bird
B a Mediterranean bird
C a kind of snake

	2

3 This speaker describes herself as an astrologer .
What point is she making?

A You have to be sensitive to see spirits.
B Cats and rabbits are afraid of black magic.
C Dogs have a sixth sense.

	3

4 Listen to this information about a future radio programme.
What will the programme be about?

A the climate of different countries
B plants and gardening in different countries
C food and clothes in different countries

	4

5 You will hear two friends talking about a recent trip.
What did the girl do on her trip?

A She looked round a modern prison.
B She looked round an old prison.
C She paid £6.00 to go to a museum.

	5

6 Two friends are talking about a match that one of them saw.
Which of these might have been the newspaper headline about this match?

A Smith the new tennis champion!
B Jones the new tennis champion!
C Smith the new golf champion!

	6

7 Listen to this person talking to a member of the public.
What is the speaker's occupation?

A a doctor
B a dentist
C a Police Officer

	7

8 Listen to this discussion between two people. They are discussing the value of something to Britain.
What is it they are disagreeing about?

A the European Union
B the Royal Family
C the rest of the world

How certain are you? Go back and look at the questions again, and decide for each one whether you are *very certain*, *fairly certain*, or *not certain*.

Answers and tapescript are on page 55.

You will hear 8 short spoken texts – each about 30 seconds long. Decide for each one whether A, B or C is the right answer.
Listen to each spoken text twice before you go on to the next one.

EXAM EXERCISE 2

1 A doctor is giving you some advice about the illness called flu.
Who does she say should be protected against flu?

A everyone
B people with heart disease, etc.
C people with a bad cold

2 An Assistant Manager is reporting an incident to his boss.
What is he accusing Michael White of doing?

A taking some boxes from the storage room
B hiding some boxes behind the stairs
C stealing some boxes that had already been unloaded

3 A Travel Agent is describing some holiday accommodation.
What kind of accommodation is it?

A a house on a hillside overlooking the sea
B two apartments with their own swimming pool
C the first floor of a house near a river

4 A jazz musician is being interviewed.
How does he feel about playing jazz on the trumpet?

A He gets bored with playing the same old tunes every night.
B He feels it is the natural instrument for him.
C He wishes he had taken up the drums.

5 Two women are discussing their friend's new baby.
What do you know about John's looks?

A His face is moon-shaped.
B He does not have black hair.
C His ears stick out.

6 An old man is remembering a journey on an ocean liner.
What happened to the piano?

A It became unfixed and travelled round the lounge for 3 days.
B A pianist played it madly for 3 days.
C No-one could stop a servant playing it.

Letts

7 A teenager is chatting to a friend.
What is he recommending?

A an island holiday
B a film
C a book

	7

8 Listen to this person telling a friend about something.
What is he describing?

A a fishing trip
B a picture
C a foggy day

	8

How certain are you of your answers: *very certain*, *fairly certain* or *not certain*?

Answers and tapescript are on page 57.

SELF ASSESSMENT

Think about the Exam Exercises that you have just done. For each of the two Exam Exercises, answer these questions to yourself:

1 How many answers did you get right?
If you got five out of eight correct, or more, then you passed that Part.

2 How many did you answer correctly that you were *very certain* about?
The more the better.

3 Did you follow some of the advice I gave to you earlier? In particular, did you:
  • read all the clue sentences and questions carefully first?
  • rewind your tape and listen to each spoken text twice before doing the next one?
  • try to imagine what was happening?
  • always remember which spoken text you were listening to and what number it was?
  • go on listening even if there was a word you didn't understand?
  • decide when to look at A, B and C?

A note about self assessment

If you tend to have the right answers for those you were *very certain* about, that is excellent – well done.

If you get the right answers, but are often *not certain*, this suggests you are either guessing (which is all right if you have to, but you don't want to do it too much), or that you are not very confident and perhaps need some further listening practice.

If you are *very certain* they are right but in fact your answers are often wrong, then perhaps you are not listening closely enough and think you know the answer a bit too soon without careful checking.

LOOKING AT PART 2

The ten questions numbered 9 - 18 form Part 2 of the Listening Paper. In the exam, you will hear the spoken text twice and the instructions are also on the tape, but the questions you have to answer are not on the tape this time. In this part you hear just one spoken text. It lasts about three minutes and may be just one person talking, or a conversation between two people. Your job is to listen and then fill in the blank boxes on your answer sheet. You have to finish a sentence, or answer a question or provide some information.

Remember that the questions are in the same order as the information in the spoken text.

ANSWERING THE QUESTIONS

The questions are not all exactly the same as each other in this part and so you will have to use a variety of skills when filling in your answers. On the left hand side of the page, there is a mixture of the following:

- questions to answer
- unfinished statements which you must complete
- some notes on what the speaker says, which need finishing.

On the right hand side of the page are ten boxes, numbered 9 - 18. You write your answers in these boxes. You don't normally need to write more than about 3 words for each answer. At the top of the page it tells you what you will hear. For example:

You will hear part of a radio talk about a foreign language course for British people.

Then it tells you to fill in the boxes 9 - 18. For example:

For questions 9 - 18, complete the notes which summarise what the speaker says. You will need to write a word or a short phrase in each box.

Filling in the answer sheet

At the end of the test, you will be given time to transfer your answers to the answer sheet (see page 78).

Note that it's always a good idea to pay careful attention to your spelling, but don't worry if you do make a mistake because you won't lose marks if it is still clear what word you meant to write. (Just occasionally, though, you may have to write a word that the speaker spells for you on the tape during the spoken text – in this case you must get it right.)

WHAT'S BEING TESTED

Like Part 1, Part 2 aims to see if you can understand the general idea of the spoken text and also some of the main points. Because it's quite a long text, taking about 3 minutes, there won't necessarily be questions on every part of it. But you will have to understand enough to summarise parts or pick out particular points of information. In addition, it may test your ability to discover the meaning of something which is not stated in a completely straightforward way. Here is a simple example: you might realise that the speaker likes water if he enjoys fishing, sailing and swimming, even though water may not actually be mentioned. This is called deducing the meaning, or deduction. We will practise all these different aspects of Part 2 in the following Practice Exercises.

PRACTICE EXERCISES

In this part you have two Practice Exercises which are quite short – about one minute long each. There are 3 boxes to fill in for each one, to help you get used to the system. To give you a little extra guidance, there is a note by each box telling you what kind of question it is. Of course in the exam you won't get this clue. Use it now to guide you to find an appropriate answer. For example, if it is a question about the general idea (called *summarising*), then think about the overall purpose and message.

If it is about a specific point (called *detail*), you will have to listen carefully for that particular piece of information to be mentioned. If it says *deduction*, you will know that the information asked for is not clearly stated in the text, but it is suggested in some way so you can work it out. *Main point* means that you must look for a point that is particularly important to the meaning of the text.

In these Practice Exercises, you will also find some extra help in the boxes. I have put in a word or two to indicate what kind of answer you should give. In the exam you don't get this help, so quite soon you will have to start thinking yourself about what sort of answer is needed.

You will notice that Practice Exercises 1 and 4 ask you to complete sentences, and Practice Exercises 2 and 3 ask questions that you must answer.

When you have had a go at Practice Exercise 1, look at the answers and study them, making sure you understand why the answers are the ones given, before doing Practice Exercise 2.

The answers, notes and tapescripts are on pages 59-61.

PRACTICE EXERCISE 1

You will hear an extract from a TV programme about shopping. Complete the notes below in the numbered boxes. A few words is enough for each.

Supermarkets are popular with

who?	**1**
	main point

A big disadvantage is

that...	**2**
	detail

In 1994 most new stores were built

where?	**3**
	main point

Now check your answers on page 59.

PRACTICE EXERCISE 2

You will hear a conversation between two friends. Write the answer to the questions below in the numbered boxes.

What do they both want to do?

verb	**1**
	summarising

How do they choose?

in an unusual way	**2**
	main point

Do they agree to go to the Angel Falls in Venezuela?

yes or no	**3**
	deduction

Now check your answers on page 59.

The next two Practice Exercises are nearly two minutes long each. They both have six questions. (Remember that the exam ones are about three minutes with ten questions each). The questions here are similar to the kind you practised in Practice Exercises 1 and 2, but you have something extra to do this time: as well as writing the answer to each question, make a note of what kind of question you think it is. Write *summarising*, *main point*, *detail* or *deduction* for each. It will then be useful for you to see if the ones you were right about were also ones you got the right answer to. A word of advice here – they may not be very evenly distributed. For example you could have lots of *detail* questions in one exercise and none in another, so don't look for an even pattern!

Again, you will find some words in the boxes to give you a clear idea of the sort of answer you should give.

You will hear two friends, Annie and Jack, discussing a cycling holiday. Answer the questions in the boxes below and decide what kind of question each one is, as suggested above.

How does Annie know about this cycling holiday?

by doing something	1

What kind of question is it?

How long is the holiday?

length of time	2

What kind of question is it?

Why might Jack be happy to hire a bike?

because his ...	3

What kind of question is it?

Can part of the holiday be by car?

yes/no	4

What kind of question is it?

What must you do in the competition?

verb	5

What kind of question is it?

What are they about to do next?

immediately	6

What kind of question is it?

Now check your answers on page 60.

You will hear some advice being given in a consumer radio programme. Complete the summarising notes and answer the questions below. (See instructions above Practice Exercise 3).

NOTES FOR NEIGHBOURS

This advice tells old people what to do when

something happens	1

What kind of question is it?

Before opening the door you should

do something	2

What kind of question is it?

and

do something else	3

What kind of question is it?

Before talking to unknown visitors, you should

do something	4

What kind of question is it?

You should never trust

something	5

What kind of question is it?

or

what kind of person?	6

What kind of question is it?

Now check your answers on page 60.

DOING THE EXAM

Try to

- keep listening hard for the whole time – three minutes is a long time, so this practice will be very helpful
- write quickly enough to keep up, but in clear enough writing so that you can read your answers when you transfer them to the answer sheet
- use correct spelling and suitable grammar, but don't worry too much, you can still get your mark if you make minor mistakes
- check that your answer makes sense, i.e. that what you write fits with the first half of the sentence or the question. It's a good idea to read through your answers carefully at the end.

Try not to put more than one answer in each box – if one is wrong, then you won't get your mark, even if the other is right.

Try not to use more than 3 or 4 words in each box.

Try not to spend so much time writing the answers that you forget to listen to the next bit.

EXAM EXERCISES

In these two Exam Exercises you will find spoken texts to listen to, each of them about the same length as the one in Part Two of the First Certificate Listening paper. There are 10 questions with each text, as there are in the exam. Look carefully at the answers to the first text before going on to the next one. As in earlier exercises, you will find some words underlined and numbered in the tapescript, indicating the parts which are especially relevant to that particular question. The type of question is not given or asked for in these exam exercises, but it is still a good idea to continue thinking about what kind of questions they are as you go along. Also you will not find any extra help in the boxes here as you have in the earlier Practice Exercises.

As in Part 1, decide how certain you are about your answers: *very certain, fairly certain* or *not certain.*

EXAM EXERCISE 1

You will hear a teenager on regional television advertising a local school's summer activity programme. Supply the information asked for in the numbered boxes.

Time of afternoon activities		1
Two non-sporting activities		2
Which weeks for outdoor adventure course?		3
The watersport and climbing instructors are		4
Are there different age-groups?		5
Cost of outdoor adventure course		6
Do what to get reduction?		7
Money back if child doesn't attend?		8
Do what to get a medal?		9
Can those on multi-activity courses buy lunch?		10

How certain are you of your answers: *very certain, fairly certain* or *not certain*?
Answers and tapescript are on page 61.

You will hear part of an interview with a doctor about food. Complete the summarising notes in the boxes below.

Having a sweet tooth means we like		1
Some say we get a sweet tooth		2
Others say we are born with		3
Evidence for this is that		4
Eating too much fat		5
and may		6
Cancers can be reduced by		7
To give unwilling children healthy food, do it without		8
Foods like chips aren't necessarily		9
What's bad for you is		10

How certain are you of your answers: *very certain*, *fairly certain* or *not certain*?
Answers and tapescript are on page 62.

SELF ASSESSMENT

Think about the Exam Exercises that you have just done. For each of the two Exam Exercises, answer these questions to yourself:

1 How many answers did you get right?
   If you got six out of ten correct, or more, then you passed that part.

2 How many did you answer correctly that you were *very certain* about?
   The more the better.

3 Did you follow some of the advice I gave to you earlier? In particular, did you:
   • manage to keep listening all the way through?
   • only write one answer in each box?
   • write a few words only each time?
   • write quickly and clearly?
   • check that your answers made sense?

Now read the *Note about Self Assesment* on page 10.

LOOKING AT PART 3

The next five questions, numbers 19 - 23, form Part 3 of the paper. This time you will hear five quite short spoken texts. They will only be about 30 seconds long, the same length as the ones in Part 1. Also like Part 1, they will have either one or two people speaking but now, although they are quite separate, they will be related in some way. For example they will all be about holidays or cars, or they will all be advertising something or all be telephone messages. In the exam, you will hear all the texts once and then, after a pause, all of them a second time.

ANSWERING THE QUESTIONS

In Part 3 you hear five spoken texts and have six statements to look at. You must decide which statement is true for which spoken text. You then put the number of the text in the box by the statement. So if you think statement B is true for text number 1, you write B in the box next to the number 1. As you will hear *five* texts, and there are *six* statements, one of the statements is extra and won't relate to anything you listen to.

Filling in the answer sheet
Again, you will have time at the end of the test to transfer your answers to the answer sheet (see page 78).

WHAT'S BEING TESTED

Exactly the same sorts of things are being tested in Part 3 as in Part 1. It's just a different style of task that you have to do. So you must be prepared to think again about any of these aspects: the general ideas, the main points, the purpose of the communication, where it's taking place, who the people are in relation to each other, how they feel or what opinions they have. Because you have had some practice with this approach in Part 1, you will probably find it a little easier now, but we will do some shorter Exercises first before trying a full exam-type question.

PRACTICE EXERCISES

All three of the Practice Exercises in this part are similar. In each of them I will present you with three short spoken texts – slightly shorter than the ones in the exam. For each set of three, you will find four statements. You must match three of these statements with the right spoken texts. One statement is extra and doesn't relate to any of the texts.

   You will find that one Practice Exercise deals with how the speakers feel about something, one deals with some important points of information – main points – and one deals with the purpose of the communication. The clue sentence and the questions themselves will give you a good indication of what aspect is being tested, so try to use all the information you are given to help you focus on the useful parts of what the speakers say.

   In each exercise, listen to all 3 spoken texts first before listening to them all a second time.

   In these Exercises, you should also say how you know that the answers are the ones you give, just as you did in Part 1. As usual, there are some comments with the answers to explain them, as well as key words underlined in the tapescript.

   The answers, notes and tapescripts are on pages 63-64.

Feelings, opinions, attitudes

You will hear three different people talking about their holiday last year. For Questions 1 - 3, choose from the list A - D what the speakers said on their return from holiday. Make a note for each box about what helped you answer the question.

A We complained to our holiday insurers.
B The swimming pool made us sick.
C We enjoyed it.
D We missed the second week of our holiday.

Speaker 1	**1**
Speaker 2	**2**
Speaker 3	**3**

Now check your answers on page 63.

Points of information

You will hear three telephone messages recorded by three different theatres. For Questions 1 - 3, choose from the list A - D what discounts are offered. Make a note for each box about what helped you answer the question.

A 50% for old age pensioners
B for someone in a wheelchair and a companion
C on two or more bookings
D for those out of work

Speaker 1	**1**
Speaker 2	**2**
Speaker 3	**3**

Now check your answers on page 63.

Purpose of the message

You will hear one conversation and two individuals talking about the British National Lottery. For Questions 1 - 3, choose from the list A - D what overall purpose the speakers have. Make a note next to each box about what helped you answer the question.

A to defend the lottery
B to advertise the lottery
C to express disapproval
D to persuade the listener to play

Number 1	**1**
Number 2	**2**
Number 3	**3**

Now check your answers on page 64.

DOING THE EXAM

Here are a few more hints. Some you will recognise from before, but I want to remind you again.

Try to
- make a mental picture of what your hear
- remember which speaker you are listening to – it's easy to get confused and write the letter in the wrong box
- keep calm – this is another long test and you must keep going.

Try not to focus on a single word – the same word may appear in more than one text, so *how it is used* is very important.

Try not to rush into listening before studying the questions carefully.

EXAM EXERCISES

In these exercises you will find five spoken texts to listen to, each of them about the same length as the ones in Part Three of the First Certificate Listening paper. As in the exam, you will need to match the answers (numbered A - F) to the right speakers. There is one extra answer which won't apply to any of the speakers, so you will have to decide which one you should leave out. As in earlier sections, you will find some words underlined in the tapescript, indicating the parts which are especially relevant to the right answer. There are no extra comments in this section, but it is still a good idea to continue thinking in detail about how you arrived at your answer.

EXAM EXERCISE 1

You will hear house sellers talking about five different properties for sale, and their location. For Questions 1 - 5, choose from the list A - F which house these different people would probably choose .

A a two-car family
B a keen footballer
C someone who works Monday to Friday in London
D a keen cyclist
E someone who likes eating out
F someone with a two-year-old child

How certain are you about your answers:
very certain, fairly certain or *not certain*?

The answers and tapescript are on page 64.

Speaker 1		1
Speaker 2		2
Speaker 3		3
Speaker 4		4
Speaker 5		5

EXAM EXERCISE 2

You will hear five different people answering the question: "What do you like about your job?". For Questions 1 - 5, choose from the list A - F which job each of the speakers does.

A a cook
B a photographer
C a dressmaker
D a painter
E a hairdresser
F a gardener

How certain are you about your answers:
very certain, fairly certain or *not certain?*

The answers and tapescript are on page 65.

Speaker 1		1
Speaker 2		2
Speaker 3		3
Speaker 4		4
Speaker 5		5

SELF ASSESSMENT

Think about the Exam Exercises that you have just done. For each of the two Exam Exercises, answer these questions to yourself:

1 How many answers did you get right?
   If you got three out of five correct, or more, then you passed that part.
2 How many did you answer correctly that you were very certain about?
   The more the better.
3 Did you follow some of the advice I gave to you earlier? In particular, did you:
   • use all the available information to help you find the answers?
   • keep calm and keep going?
   • always remember who was speaking?
   • listen for complete ideas, rather than single words?

Now read the *Note about Self Assessment* on page 10.

LOOKING AT PART 4

Questions 24 - 30 are the last seven questions in the Listening Paper. Once again, like Part 2, you have to listen to one spoken text that lasts about 3 minutes. You will not know beforehand exactly what kind of questions there will be, but they will be one of three types:

1 They could be Multiple Choice, (from A, B or C), like the questions in Part 1.
2 You might find 7 statements and you must say if each one is true or false.
3 You may have to decide on who said something, felt something, wants to do something, etc.

We will practise all of these different questions in this part.

ANSWERING THE QUESTIONS

The questions will be very clear, as they are in the other parts.

In the case of deciding who did what, etc. you choose between three possible people and write their first letter (which they will tell you) in the right box. Write your answer clearly, so you can read it at the end of the test.

Filling in the answer sheet

Again, you will have time at the end of the test to transfer your answers to the answer sheet. Make sure you copy exactly what you wrote on the question sheet.

WHAT'S BEING TESTED

The 3-minute spoken text will either be a conversation or one person speaking. As in the other parts, you hear it twice.

This part may test
• your understanding of the general idea of the text
• your ability to pick out the main points
• your ability to pick out details
• your ability to deduce meaning. Remember, this is when the information asked for is not clearly stated in the text, but it is suggested in some way so you can work it out.

PRACTICE EXERCISES

We will start with three short exercises of the *Who did what?* kind. They are not very difficult and only have 3 questions each (seven in the exam, remember), but they will get you used to this kind of question. Practice Exercise 4 is a straightforward Multiple Choice task and Practice Exercises 5 and 6 introduce you to the True/False kind of question. Remember that more than one of the statements *may* be true.

Listen to the spoken text twice. Leave a brief pause between each listening.

The answers, notes and tapescripts are on pages 67-69.

PRACTICE EXERCISE 1

Who did what?

You will hear two friends talking about something that happened at a local restaurant recently. You will hear them mention Helen, Mike and the restaurant owner, among other people. In each numbered box write one of these letters:

H Helen   **M** Mike   **O** Owner of Restaurant

Read through the questions carefully before listening.

1 Who did the Policeman want to talk to?

	1

2 Who had had an accident?

	2

3 Who wanted to talk to the Police?

	3

Now check your answers on page 67.

PRACTICE EXERCISE 2

Who did what?

You will hear Chris and his Dad telling Chris's Mum about what Benji, the dog, did. In each numbered box write one of these letters:

C Chris   **D** Dad   **M** Mum

Read through the questions carefully before listening.

1 Who guessed something?

	1

2 Who is frightened about something?

	2

3 Who is willing to talk to the farmer?

	3

Now check your answers on page 67.

PRACTICE EXERCISE 3

Who did what?

You will hear a group of students who share a flat discussing what's going to happen tonight. In each numbered box write one of these letters:

J Jane   **D** Dave   **A** Andy

Read through the questions carefully before listening.

1 Who feels guilty about something?

	1

2 Who is looking forward to something ?

	2

3 Who is not happy about something?

	3

Now check your answers on page 68.

PRACTICE EXERCISE 4

Multiple choice

Listen to Gail and David arguing about something of Gail's.
What are they talking about?

A a photo
B a diary entry
C a letter

Now check your answers on page 68.

True/false

You will hear a mother describing a strange event.
Decide if these statements are **true** or **false**.
Write the letter **T** for **true** or **F** for **false** in each box.

1 Sarah felt very cold.

2 She thought she saw an enormous bird.

3 The officials don't believe it was dangerous.

	1
	2
	3

Now check your answers on page 68.

True/false

You will hear someone telling you about an accident.
Decide if these statements are **true** or **false**.
Write the letter **T** for **true** or **F** for **false** in each box.

1 Everybody on the plane was killed.

2 There's a body still there.

3 A plane crashed near a lake.

	1
	2
	3

Now check your answers on page 69.

DOING THE EXAM

Here is my last list of hints on how to approach the Listening Paper. Most of them are
repetitions of earlier advice but it is worth saying them again. When you are doing Part 4:

Try to
- use the information you are given about the speakers, etc. to help you imagine the scene
- always know who you are listening to
- keep calm and keep going – 3 minutes is quite a long time
- follow all the advice I've given you in this book!

Try not to worry if you don't catch everything first time – this can easily happen, especially if
it's a conversation.
Try not to be distracted by wrong answers (A,B,C) in the Multiple Choice questions – focus
more on the question first.
Try not to make any of the mistakes you've made before!

EXAM EXERCISES

Remember to consider how certain you are about your answers: *very certain, fairly certain* or
not certain.

EXAM EXERCISE 1

You will hear two friends talking about computers and the Internet and the sort of people who use it. Their names are Bob and Liz. In each numbered box write one of these letters:

L Liz
B Bob
A Another Internet user

1 Who is embarrassed about something? `1`

2 Who is surprised about something? `2`

3 Who likes to be an independent traveller? `3`

4 Who does Liz want answers from? `4`

5 Who doesn't intend to change his/her mind? `5`

6 Who is going to India? `6`

7 Who recommends the old city of Delhi? `7`

How certain are you about your answers: *very certain, fairly certain* or *not certain*?

Answers and tapescript are on page 69.

EXAM EXERCISE 2

You will hear a TV journalist, Max Wing, asking John Walker about his work helping the British river bird, the swan. In each numbered box write **A**, **B** or **C**.

1 Where do you find swans?
A on all British rivers
B on most British rivers `1`
C on a few British rivers

2 Why do the swans get injured?
A because their necks get caught in the bushes
B because they swallow fishing equipment `2`
C because they eat polluted fish

3 How many injured swans die each year?
A three quarters of all swans
B 1100 `3`
C more than 1100

4 What happens 6 times a day?
A surgery on baby swans
B half the baby swans die `4`
C baby swans come in with hooks in their throats

5 The Helpline telephone number is
A expensive
B free `5`
C cheap

6 What is the Helpline telephone number ?
A 0980 564979
B 0980 554797 `6`
C 0980 934757

7 Whose fault is it that swans get sick?

A all fishermen

B a few fishermen

C most fishermen

How certain are you about your answers: *very certain*, *fairly certain* or *not certain*?

Answers and tapescript are on page 70.

SELF ASSESSMENT

Think about the Exam Exercises that you have just done. For each of the two Exam Exercises, answer these questions to yourself:

1 How many answers did you get right?
  If you got five out of seven correct, or more, then you passed that part.

2 How many did you answer correctly that you were very certain about?
  More than in the other three parts, I hope.

3 Did you follow some of the advice I gave to you earlier? In particular, did you:
  * focus on the context and questions before the multiple choice statements?
  * imagine the scene as you were listening?
  * always know who was speaking ?
  * keep calm, especially if you didn't understand something?
  * feel all your efforts in using this book have been worthwhile!

Now read the *Note about Self Assessment* on page 10.

Good luck with the Trial Paper.

Before you begin, read about the cassette in 'Trial Paper' on page 2. Now begin playing the cassette.

PART 1

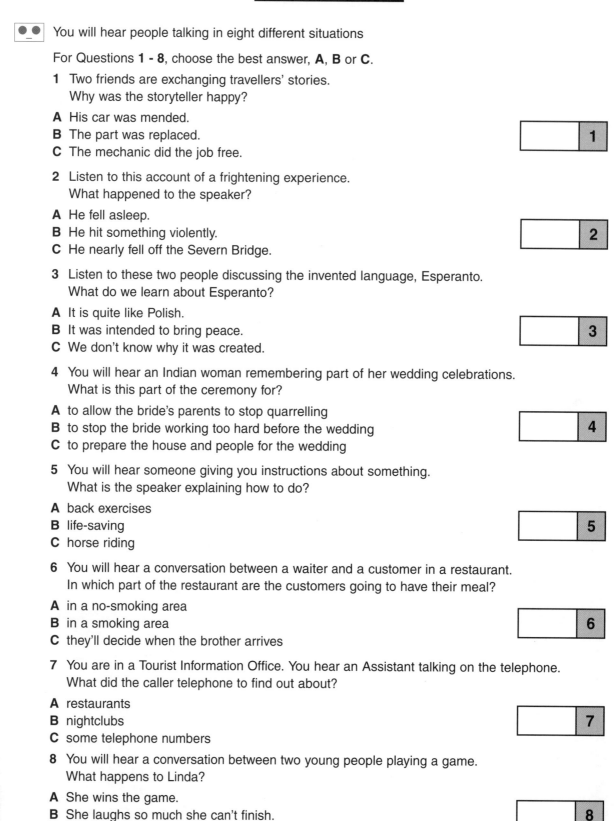

You will hear people talking in eight different situations

For Questions **1 - 8**, choose the best answer, **A**, **B** or **C**.

1 Two friends are exchanging travellers' stories.
Why was the storyteller happy?

A His car was mended.
B The part was replaced.
C The mechanic did the job free.

1

2 Listen to this account of a frightening experience.
What happened to the speaker?

A He fell asleep.
B He hit something violently.
C He nearly fell off the Severn Bridge.

2

3 Listen to these two people discussing the invented language, Esperanto.
What do we learn about Esperanto?

A It is quite like Polish.
B It was intended to bring peace.
C We don't know why it was created.

3

4 You will hear an Indian woman remembering part of her wedding celebrations.
What is this part of the ceremony for?

A to allow the bride's parents to stop quarrelling
B to stop the bride working too hard before the wedding
C to prepare the house and people for the wedding

4

5 You will hear someone giving you instructions about something.
What is the speaker explaining how to do?

A back exercises
B life-saving
C horse riding

5

6 You will hear a conversation between a waiter and a customer in a restaurant.
In which part of the restaurant are the customers going to have their meal?

A in a no-smoking area
B in a smoking area
C they'll decide when the brother arrives

6

7 You are in a Tourist Information Office. You hear an Assistant talking on the telephone.
What did the caller telephone to find out about?

A restaurants
B nightclubs
C some telephone numbers

7

8 You will hear a conversation between two young people playing a game.
What happens to Linda?

A She wins the game.
B She laughs so much she can't finish.
C She loses the game.

8

PART 2

You will hear a young woman, Julie, describing to a local journalist a car accident she had recently. For Questions **9 - 18**, fill in the information asked for by the news reporter. You will need to write a word or a short phrase in each box.

Day of accident	9
Colour and type of Julie's car	10
Position of red car	11
Why didn't the other driver stop?	12
Driver of other car agreed he was	13
Julie went to	14
The Police asked questions and checked	15
Where was the owner of the other car?	16
The other driver is an employee at	17
Julie feels lucky because	18

PART 3

You will hear five people reading out short articles from a newspaper. For Questions **19 - 23**, choose from the list **A - F** which statement is true in which story. Use the letters only once. Remember that there is one extra statement which you do not need to use.

A Something might close down.

B Something has been removed.

C Something has closed.

D Something is opening.

E Something will close and will open again.

F Something will never close.

Speaker 1		19
Speaker 2		20
Speaker 3		21
Speaker 4		22
Speaker 5		23

PART 4

You will hear a conversation between Mrs Nelson and a visitor to her house. You will also hear Diana and Mr Nelson. For Questions **24 - 30**, decide which of the choices **A**, **B**, or **C** is the correct answer.

24 Annie has come
A for the first time.
B by air.
C by boat.

| | 24 |

25 How many children have the Nelsons got?
A 3
B 4
C 5

| | 25 |

26 Annie has come to
A help with the business.
B look after the children.
C study music.

| | 26 |

27 Ben and Andrew
A left the cat out.
B gave their pie to the cat.
C forgot to cover the pie.

| | 27 |

28 The number of family members Annie meets is
A 3
B 4
C 5

| | 28 |

29 What do the Nelsons live in?
A a town flat
B a house with a garden
C a cottage in the country

| | 29 |

30 Who feels pleased to see her violin?
A Mrs Nelson
B Diana
C Mr Nelson

| | 30 |

The complete tapescript for the Trial Paper is on pages 71-77. The answers are on page 77.

LOOKING AT PART 1

Part 1 of the Speaking Paper lasts about 4 minutes. During these 4 minutes the interlocutor will interview you in an informal way, by asking you questions about yourself. (The interlocutor is the person who talks to a candidate during an exam. On page 2 of the Introduction I have explained this more fully.) You should answer the questions and, where you can, give a bit of extra information or your own ideas and opinions. In this part the conversation is just between you and an interlocutor. No-one else will take part in your conversation. But the assessor will be present and will be listening and marking your performance. Some of the questions will be very simple like *Where are you from?* and others will be a little more complicated and open, like *What are your plans for the future?* Clearly you will want to say more about your plans than about where you're from. I will give a few hints later about how you might approach these different sorts of questions. Meanwhile, remember that the general areas that you should be ready to talk about are these:

- personal information
- your present circumstances
- your past experiences
- your future plans.

WHAT'S BEING TESTED

While you are talking to the interlocutor, the assessor will be listening to you. If you don't say enough, it will be very difficult to give you a fair mark, so in order to pass, you must speak enough and also clearly and loudly enough for both the interlocutor and assessor to hear you properly. In a speaking test like this, there is no right or wrong answer – there are lots of possibilities, but of course some answers are better than others. There are 4 main areas that the assessor will be looking at and marking:

- your use of grammar
- your use of vocabulary
- your pronunciation
- your interactive communication – this means your ability to make it clear what you mean (even if you don't know all the right words and grammar). I'll give you some help with this in a moment.

DOING THE EXAM

Here are some hints for you to think about to help you with Part 1 of the Speaking Paper.

Try to
- smile and look confident (even if you don't feel it!)
- remember to say Hello when you go into the exam room
- concentrate on what is said to you
- look at the person you're talking to
- ask for explanation if you don't understand something
- add a little bit to your answers where you can.

Try not to say one word and then stop.

Try not to worry if you have to ask for repetition – remember it's your speaking that's on test, not your listening. The interlocutor will try and help you Understand as much as possible.

Try not to speak too quietly.

Try not to learn speeches off by heart.

PRACTICE EXERCISE

Below are some questions like the ones the interlocutor might ask you. This is what I suggest you do if you can: ask a friend to put the questions to you and record the conversation that you have. It should take about 4 minutes altogether, but that's not very important for this exercise. Then look at the *Useful Language* section and if you think you could do better, do the exercise again, using some of the language you find there.

Here are some practice questions:
- Where do you come from?
- Where were you born?
- Did you go to school there?
- Is it a nice place to live?
- Is there much opportunity to practise your English there?
- What do you hope to do in the next few years?

When you have tried answering the Practice Questions once, have a look through the next section.

PRACTICE EXERCISE

Where do you come from?
You could say:

- *I come from Prague, the capital of the Czech Republic. Do you know it?*
- *I come from Hungary originally, but now I live in Switzerland, in Geneva.*

Do not say:'I am coming from.....' (This means that you will be on your way from there to somewhere else in the near future! e.g. *I'm coming from Tokyo on Friday – will you meet me at the airport?*)

USEFUL LANGUAGE

Where were you born?
You could say:

- *I was born in Helsinki, in the middle of winter.*
- *I was born in Mexico City, but my brothers and sisters were all born in Guadalajara, which is further north.*

Do not say: 'I am born in...' or 'I born in....' (These are both grammatically incorrect.)

Did you go to school there?
You could say:

- *Well, I went to my first school there, till I was 9 years old. After that I moved schools and went to ...*
- *Yes, I was at Primary and Secondary School there, and took my............... exams there too.*

Do not say: 'Yes'. (This isn't enough.)

Is it a nice place to live?
You could say:

- *In some ways yes and in some ways no. It's very beautiful, especially in summer, but it gets very crowded, with tourists. There's a lot for young people to do, and I have lots of friends there, but it's difficult to find a good job.*
- *Sometimes I like it, but it's rather quiet. It's a lovely place to go home to at weekends or for holidays, but I'd prefer to live and work somewhere bigger.*

Remember that there is usually a negative adjective after the word r*ather*: e.g. *rather cold, rather big, rather noisy*. This suggests you don't like it being cold, big or noisy.

Do not say: 'Yes, I like.'(You must always put another word after *like*. e.g. *I like it.*)
  'Is a pretty place.' (You must always put a subject with the verb. e.g. *It is a pretty place.*)
  'I'd rather prefer...' (If you are choosing one of two things, it's better to say: *I prefer...* + noun, or *I'd prefer to ...* + verb.)

Is there much opportunity to practise your English there?

You could say:

- *Yes there is. I'm lucky because I have some English-speaking friends I can talk to, and there are also a number of good evening classes available.*
- *Unfortunately not. Most people who want to learn English have to go to another town or they go abroad. Of course you can learn on your own with books and tapes, but it's much more difficult.*

Do not say: 'There is not many English peoples to speak with.' (This should be: *There aren't many English speakers to talk to.*)

What do you hope to do in the next few years?

You could say:

- *I'm not at all sure, but I hope to get a job where I can use my languages, and perhaps travel.*
- *If I pass First Certificate, I'm planning to do Proficiency next, and then I'd like to work in business. I'm particularly interested in working with computers.*

Do not say: 'I think I go to university.' or 'I think to get married.' (These are both incorrect grammatically. It is better to say: *I'm thinking of going to university, to study...(law)* or *'I'm thinking of getting married.'*)

SELF ASSESSMENT

Think about the Practice Exercise that you have just done. Now answer these questions to yourself:

1 Which questions did you answer best? In what way? Think about your grammar, vocabulary and pronunciation as well as getting your message understood.

2 What areas do you need to improve?

3 Did you follow some of the advice I gave to you earlier? In particular, did you:
- start your conversation looking confident?
- ask if you didn't understand something?
- look at the person you were talking to?
- give long enough answers to make a proper conversation?
- speak clearly?
- repeat the exercise using some of the help in the *Useful Language* section?

Exam tip

In the exam the conversation will flow like a real one, so the questions you get may build on the answers you have already given. You must listen for the connections and make your replies fit them in a natural way. For example:

Q: *Where do you live?*
A: *I live in Bonn, but I used to live in Hamburg.*
Q: *Did you like it there?*

There are two things to think about when you answer the second question here:

1 *there* means *Hamburg*, not Bonn, because *Did* is past tense, so the reply should be about Hamburg, not Bonn.

2 You could start your reply with a short form: *Yes I did* or *No I didn't.* It's always important to listen out for the auxiliary (e.g. *did*) so that you can use the right short form in your reply.

LOOKING AT PART 2

Part 2 takes 4 minutes. You do this part with another candidate, but you don't have a conversation with them. What you have to do during that time is talk for one minute about two photographs that the interlocutor will show you, and then for twenty seconds about two photographs that the other candidate has. You will find that there are precise instructions about what kind of thing you should talk about and when you should do this. In general the photographs you are given will be related in some way, (e.g. different places to have a meal, or different jobs that people do) and you will be asked to compare and contrast the photos before giving your own opinion about which you prefer or find more attractive. The other candidate will then briefly give their opinion about your pictures. Then the other candidate will talk about a different pair of photos and then you will be asked to add your own opinion about them – taking about 20 seconds.

WHAT'S BEING TESTED

During the time you are talking about the pictures, the assessor will expect you to give information and express your opinions through comparing and contrasting them and any ideas that they give you. Particular features of your speaking that will be marked are these:

* how much sense it makes
* how well you organise your language and ideas
* your use of vocabulary
* how clear your message is.

DOING THE EXAM

Below is an example of the conversation you will have with the interlocutor. In it are all the instructions you will receive so it is worth reading it carefully twice. The first time you read it, imagine that you are Candidate A. The second time, imagine you are Candidate B. That way you can get a clear picture of what you would have to do in either situation. You probably won't know until the last minute whether you are Candidate A or B, so it is sensible to be prepared to be either.

Remember that when you talk for a minute about your photos, the assessor expects to hear you comparing the pictures and what is in them before you give your own opinion. In your twenty-second turn you only need to give your views, rather than discuss the pictures in any detail .

Interlocutor Now, I'm going to give each of you two different photographs. I'd like you both to show each other your pictures and then talk about them.

You each have only one minute for this, so don't worry if I interrupt you.

Candidate A, here are your two pictures. Please let Candidate B see them. They show different school classrooms and teaching methods.

The interlocutor will now give picture sheet 1 to Candidate A.

Candidate B, I'll give you your pictures in a minute.

Candidate A, I'd like you to compare and contrast these pictures saying how you feel about schoolchildren learning in small independent groups or together in class with the teacher talking at the front.

Remember Candidate A, you have about a minute for this. All right?

Candidate A *Approximately one minute to speak*

Interlocutor Thank you. So, which school classroom would you prefer, Candidate B?

Candidate B *Approximately twenty seconds to speak*

Interlocutor Thank you. Now, Candidate B, here are your pictures. Please let Candidate A see them. They show different kinds of fun activity.

> *Interlocutor hands over picture sheet 2 to Candidate B.*

I'd like you to compare and contrast these pictures saying which leisure activity you prefer and why.

Remember Candidate B, you have about a minute for this. All right?

Candidate B *Approximately one minute to speak*

Interlocutor Thank you. Now can you tell us which activity looks the more attractive to you, Candidate A?

Candidate A *Approximately twenty seconds to speak*

Interlocutor Thank you.

PRACTICE EXERCISES

In Practice Exercise 1 you have two photographs to look at. Your task here will be to think about the kind of language and ideas you need for your one minute's speaking.

In Practice Exercise 2 there will be four photographs. You will talk for one minute about the first two and for twenty seconds about the second two. Timing yourself in each case will give you an idea of how long each part should take. (There is also an opportunity to talk for one minute about the second pair of photos at the end.)

If you can tape record your speaking and listen to it before having another go, you will find this very helpful. Look at the *Useful Language* section in each exercise after your first attempt, then record yourself again and see how much you have improved.

PRACTICE EXERCISE 1

Look at the photographs of two different schoolrooms opposite. Start by talking about what's different in the pictures, and what is similar. Think about these questions:

What are the two classrooms like?
What are the pupils doing in each one?
Do the rooms look different in any way?

Now move on to this sort of question and give your opinions with reasons:

Which kind of classroom is more like the school you went to?
In what way?
Which system is better?
Is a mixture a good idea?
Why? Is one system better for a particular age group?
Does small-group learning suit some subjects better than others? Why?
Are there any more comments you can make on how the two methods of education compare with each other? (i.e. which is better and why?)

Finally think about your own preferences:

Which system do you prefer for yourself? In what circumstances? Why?

USEFUL LANGUAGE

In all three *Useful Language* sections in this part you will find examples of language that you can use and adapt when talking about the pictures. They don't all give the same opinion, of course, and they don't follow on from each other as your speaking must. They are just a collection of different possibilities.

I have underlined words which indicate comparison or contrast.

Comparing what is in the pictures

* *In both pictures there is a maths lesson going on – you can tell that from the blackboard in the top one and the calculator in the bottom one.*
* *In the first picture the teacher is standing at the front of the class giving a maths lesson whereas in the other one a group of pupils are working on a maths problem on their own, without the teacher.*
* *In the first one some pupils have their hands up, which suggests that they can't speak without permission, while in the other one they can talk to each other when they like.*
* *With the teacher by the blackboard everyone is looking at her and learning the same thing at once. The small group, on the other hand, may be doing something different from the rest of the class.*
* *In the top picture they are all learning from the teacher, but in the other one they are learning from each other and by doing a task.*

Your opinion with reasons

* *I went to a school where they used a mixture of both methods, which I think was good because a teacher knows more about the subject than the pupils so she has to tell them about it. Then we used to go into independent groups to work on what she had just explained to us. This worked quite well.*
* *On the other hand, in a big class with a teacher, students may get bored if the teacher isn't that interesting.*
* *Although pupils in small groups may not be bored, they can start talking too much and not actually get any of the work done. Not only that, the teacher can only talk to one group at a time, so if you need her, you have to wait.*
* *Groupwork is not as good for older students, especially if they are the sort of people who don't like working with other people, although I suppose in fact it can help them learn how to work better with others, so even if they don't like it, it is good for them.*
* *One problem with small groups is that it could be that just one or two people may be left to do all the work while the others sit back not doing anything, either because they don't understand or they can't be bothered. In both cases it means they won't learn anything.*
* *Small group work is very good for language study or subjects where you have to solve problems or discuss difficult questions, but you still need the teacher to come and listen or help.*

Your personal preference

* *I think I probably learn more with the teacher at the front because you have to concentrate, but it's usually more fun to be in a group even though you might not get so much done.*

PRACTICE EXERCISE 2

In this exercise you will see two pairs of photographs. You are Candidate A. Follow these steps:

1 Read through the conversation with the Interlocutor opposite.
2 Imagine you are Candidate A preparing to talk for one minute about the first pair of photographs (the fun activity pictures on page 36).
3 Speak for one minute and try and time yourself as well as recording your speaking.
4 You are still Candidate A. Imagine that Candidate B has talked for one minute about the second pair of photographs (the music pictures on page 37).
5 Now you talk for twenty seconds about the music pictures, in answer to the Interlocutor's question "Now can you tell us which kind of music you prefer, Candidate A?". Record and time yourself if possible.

It would be good practice after that to do Candidate B's one-minute speaking task on the music pictures too, even though you have already talked about them for 20 seconds. I have given some suggestions for this in the *Useful Language* section.

Interlocutor Now, I'm going to give each of you two different photographs. I'd like you both to show each other your pictures and then talk about them.
You each have only one minute for this, so don't worry if I interrupt you.
Candidate A, here are your two pictures. Please let Candidate B see them. They show two different kinds of fun activity – fishing and riding on a roller coaster.

The interlocutor will now give picture sheet 1 to Candidate A.

Candidate B, I'll give you your pictures in a minute.
Candidate A, I'd like you to compare and contrast these pictures saying how you feel about these different activities. Remember Candidate A, you have about a minute for this. All right?

Candidate A *Approximately one minute to speak*

Interlocutor Thank you. So, which activity would you prefer, Candidate B?

Candidate B *Approximately twenty seconds to speak*

Interlocutor Thank you. Now, Candidate B, here are your pictures. Please let Candidate A see them. They show two different kinds of music being performed.

Interlocutor hands over picture sheet 2 to Candidate B.

I'd like you to compare and contrast these pictures saying which music you prefer and why.

Remember Candidate B, you have about a minute for this. All right?

Candidate B *Approximately one minute to speak*

Interlocutor Thank you. Now can you tell us which kind of music you prefer, Candidate A?

Candidate A *Approximately twenty seconds to speak*

Interlocutor Thank you.

I have underlined some of the most useful words and phrases.

USEFUL LANGUAGE

Comparing the fun activity pictures

- *There are two pictures – <u>one of a man out fishing</u> on a nice peaceful day, it looks like, and <u>one of lots of people screaming</u> on a roller coaster.*
- *<u>The only thing similar</u> about these two pictures is that they're both fun activities. <u>Apart from that,</u> they're completely different.*

Your opinion and reasons

- *A roller coaster is fast, it's fun and really exciting. And it doesn't last long, <u>whereas with</u> fishing you need a lot more patience and it's not fast and thrilling <u>at all</u> – <u>unless</u> you catch a big fish.*
- *But they can both <u>be really fun</u> if you enjoy them.*
- *You mustn't mind swinging round violently or going suddenly <u>up and down</u> or being <u>turned upside down</u>. Some people find it <u>makes them feel sick</u> so fishing would definitely be better for them.*
- *Others <u>find it</u> too frightening and feel safer <u>staying upright</u> on the ground.*

Your personal preference

- *<u>It's hard to say</u> which I prefer because they're so different.*
- *<u>It depends</u> what I feel like. <u>I'd quite like to go</u> on a roller coaster – it would <u>make a change from fishing</u>, which I often do.*
(Remember the patterns that go with the verb *depend: it depends + how, what, why, where, when, who, which; it depends on + noun; it depends whether + verb.*)

- *Personally I find that roller coasters are far more interesting and fun than fishing. Fishing is rather slow and dull – and you don't know if you're going to catch anything, but on a roller coaster you know what to expect every time, which is always really good.*

Examples of language for the one-minute talk about the music pictures:

- *One type of music shown is an orchestra with an opera singer, singing classical music, and the other picture is of a rock band playing modern music.*
- *Rock music is very different from classical music because they are so many years apart.*
- *Lots of people like different types of music. Young people seem to like rock a lot more than classical music and older people are fairly mixed.*
- *Classical music is usually a lot longer, which is one reason why some people might not like it so much. A rock song is about 5 minutes and a classical music piece is often half an hour.*
- *Another difference is that rock music usually has a beat, with a guitar playing, and there are many more instruments in an orchestra.*
- *In this orchestra there are about 100 people playing in it and an opera singer who sings in a very different way to a lead singer in a rock band. In a rock band there are usually only 4 or 5 people accompanying the singer.*
- *You don't often get quiet rock music– most of it is very loud whereas in classical music, some of it is loud but a lot more is quiet.*
- *I play the violin and I like classical music because, if you're musical, it's got a lot in it, but rock music can be interesting to listen to because it's faster and louder and more exciting.*
- *The music that appeals most to me is definitely rock music because I find the beat in lots of songs really makes you want to dance and gets you into the song, whereas with classical music it's often quite boring, but it depends how I'm feeling.*
- *Rock music is more modern and there's lots of it around, so I'm more used to it and I find opera, while it's probably more musical, is quite difficult to enjoy.*

SELF ASSESSMENT

Think about the Practice Exercises that you have just done. Did you follow some of the advice I gave to you earlier? In particular, did you:

- tape record yourself speaking, read the *Useful Language* section, then try again?
- organise your speaking well, e.g. by following the pattern of comparing the pictures first, then giving your opinions with reasons, followed by your personal preference?
- use suitable language for comparing and contrasting?
- make good sense as you were speaking?
- say most of what you wanted to say within one minute?

Exam tip

- Remember not to describe each picture separately – your task is to compare the two.
- Be prepared to talk about topics such as: sport, travel, different countries, food and restaurants, jobs, housing, hobbies, the environment.
- Practise talking about other pictures for one minute, remembering to pick out both similarities and differences.

LOOKING AT PART 3

Part 3 lasts about 3 minutes. You will be talking to another candidate about something that the interlocutor will give you – usually a diagram or drawing or something similar. You will have to use this together to do an activity like solving a problem, planning something or making a decision. Three minutes doesn't sound very long for a conversation, but remember that you must show that you can carry on talking fluently and responding sensibly to the other person in a way that will make the assessor consider that you speak good English.

WHAT'S BEING TESTED

While you and the other candidate are having your discussion, the assessor will be listening to YOU and looking out for a number of different skills. Firstly he or she will see how well you can do the following sorts of things:

- exchange information and opinions
- give reasons for what you say
- agree and disagree
- suggest ideas and thoughts
- take turns in the conversation.

As before, your grammar, vocabulary, pronunciation and fluency will all be important for your final mark.

DOING THE EXAM

Here are some hints for you to think about to help you with Part 3 of the Speaking Paper.

Try to
- listen to what the other speaker says, and use it in your replies
- keep the conversation going
- suggest ideas and also be open to the other person's opinions
- say what you mean – use different words to explain if you've forgotten the right word
- ask the other speaker what they think and if they agree with you from time to time
- summarise what you have both said so far and suggest moving on.

Try not to interrupt the other speaker too much.
Try not to talk at the same time as the other speaker – take proper turns.
Try not to worry if you can't agree – it won't matter as long as you make suggestions and listen to each other's point of view.
Try not to leave periods of silence.

PRACTICE EXERCISES

There are three Practice Exercises for you to look at and try in this part. As in Parts 1 and 2, if you can find a friend to do them with, it would be very helpful. Again if you can record your conversations and listen to them carefully afterwards to see how you might improve, this will be very valuable to you. For each of them, once you have had a first go, look at the *Useful Language* sections and then have another try a little later to see if you can do it better. Some of the *Useful Language* in each Exercise you will also be able to use in the other Practice Exercises of course, so that by the time you do Practice Exercise 3, you should find it much easier. The

Useful Language section for Practice Exercise 1 looks at how you manage your conversation – with examples of some different kinds of language that you need for the different purposes you have in the conversation, such as starting off, agreeing and disagreeing, and so on. The *Useful Language* section for Practice Exercise 2 looks particularly at some grammar patterns that you will need for Part 3, and the *Useful Language* section for Practice Exercise 3 helps you to think about *what* you can say about the topic, not just *how* you can say it. In all three Practice Exercises though, you should think about your purpose, grammar, pronunciation and the content of what you are saying. Remember that each conversation should take about 3 minutes.

PRACTICE EXERCISE 1

I'd like you to imagine that a new Wildlife Centre is being planned. There are 7 kinds of animal available but there is only enough space in the centre for 5 kinds of animal. The 7 kinds are:

brown bears • elephants • monkeys • tigers • crocodiles • tropical birds • deer

Below is a plan of the space available. Find another person to talk to if you can and decide together which area would be suitable for which kind of animal and why. You will also have to decide which two to leave out and why.

Focus on managing the conversation

In any conversation we must take turns to speak. It is important to understand when to speak and when to listen. Every time someone speaks, they have a purpose. The language I have listed below is designed to help you think about what you should be doing during your discussion, and to give you some ideas about how you can do it. This language is useful for any situation and so you should remind yourself of it before doing the other Practice Exercises too. Of course there are many other ways of doing these things. These are just a few ideas.

Starting off
* *So what we've got is ... (five areas and seven kinds of animal.)*
* *Shall we start by thinking about ... (the lake?)*
* *I think...(elephants would be the easiest one to begin with because they'll need a huge area...)*

Saying what you think
* *I think....* • *Another idea would be to...*
* Simply make a statement: e.g. *Monkeys like swinging from tree to tree so there would have to be a high fence to stop them escaping.* or: *Elephants also like mud to roll in.*
* *I still think...* (if the other speaker has not persuaded you to change your mind)
* *It seems to me that* + statement

Giving or adding reasons
* *We'll leave out the tigers and deer* (NB. The plural of *deer* is *deer*) *because ... all the others seem to fit the areas better.*
* *That's a good idea – I've seen it before (in a zoo).*
* Using *with:* e.g. *This space would be best for the birds, with its enclosed cage.*

Wondering
* *I wonder if... (bears like caves).*
* *I suppose they might... (escape if the fence isn't high enough).*
* *I was thinking that ... (it might be possible to put the deer round the lake).*
* *On top of that* (meaning: *not only that...*) *... (the tigers might be difficult to see).*
* *The same thing applies to ... (the deer).*

Agreeing
* *I think you're right...* • *I think so too* • *I would go along with you ...*
* *All right* • *OK* • *I agree with you* (or *I agree with that idea*)
* *Yes* + extra reason e.g. *they'd like the trees too.*
* *No* (after negative statement): e.g. Speaker 1: *"You can't put birds in an open space."* Speaker 2: *"No, you can't."*
  This is an important point to remember in English: If you agree with something negative, you say *No*.
* Finishing another speaker's sentence if they get stuck, e.g. Speaker 1: *"the lake would be ....."* Speaker 2: *"good for crocodiles."*
* *Yes*, (then say the same thing in different words)

Asking for opinion or agreement
* *Do you think ... (bears would live in a pit?)*
* *Would you agree ...?* (Very polite) • *Don't you think that ... ?*
* *What do you feel about ... ?* • *What about you ...?*
* Use question tag at end of sentence, e.g. *....don't you?/ isn't it?/ wouldn't they?/ mightn't they ?*

Disagreeing
* *It's true that... (monkeys like trees, but they could escape)* • *I don't really agree...*
* *It depends ... (how tall the fence is)* • *On the other hand ...*

Clarifying and asking for clarification
* *Do you mean...?* • *What I mean is ...* • *So you're suggesting that ... ?*
* *Are you saying that ... ?* • *It depends what you mean by ....*
* *I can't remember the word but it looks like ... /...it means ... /... it's what you do when...*

41

Moving the conversation on
- Mention something and ask question about it: e.g. *A wooded area with a high fence – would monkeys like that?* or: *The pit – do you think deer would be happy in a pit?*
- *Let's see, what about ... (the birds?)* • *Do you think ...(elephants can swim?)* • *Also, ...*
- *Or you could ...* • *What do you think about ...?* • *But there's also the question of ...*

Bringing the conversation back to the task
- *But it says we have to.....* • *We've got to decide....*
- *So what we've decided so far is...* • *Right, so I think...*
- *There's also the question of ...* • *We haven't discussed ... yet, have we?*

PRACTICE EXERCISE 2

Here are three maps. In each one is a house marked with a *. One of these three houses is to be offered as a holiday house to overseas visitors in July and August each year. Decide which you think would be most popular and why.

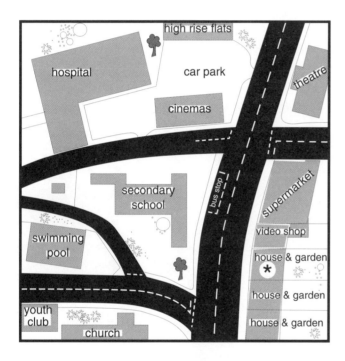
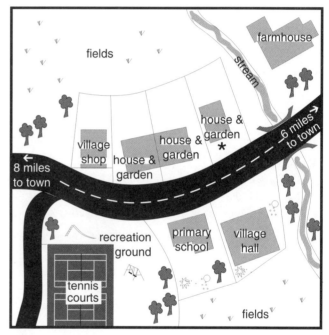
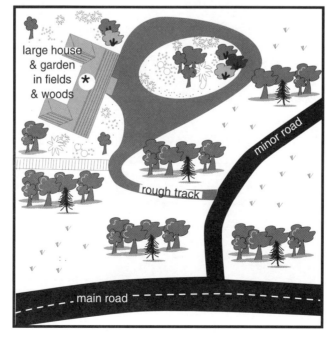

Focus on grammar

It is very difficult to say exactly what grammar you will need when you don't know what the exam discussion will be about or who you will be talking to. However, there are certain areas which are very important to be strong on. These discussions always ask you to form opinions about something which hasn't yet been decided on. This means that you are often talking about suggestions, not facts. For this you need words like: _would_, _might_ and _could_. For example, all the following sentences were said in one 3-minute conversation by English speakers when I asked them to discuss the question in this Practice Exercise. (They are not in any particular order.) They are all sentences which you could use in this one, or adapt to other similar conversations:

- _I think people might like the country house best._
- _Younger people might think it was boring._
- _Yes, they might prefer this one on the High Street._
- _Older adults might hate it because it would be too noisy._
- _Younger children would enjoy the countryside and wouldn't be so bothered about the town attractions._
- _That would be less appealing._
- _If they didn't like the town, they might enjoy the village._
- _A carpark would be useful for the parents._
- _A house in the town would be pretty popular with students, with a Youth Club right opposite._
- _The large house and garden might be good for older adults or with young children._
- _It would be less dangerous._
- _People could have a gentle game of tennis or they could go to the recreation ground._
- _More age groups would prefer the town, if it was a nice town._
- _It's only a 6-mile drive to town, which would suit all ages._
- _In the country – that could be a bit too isolated for many people._
- _The town would be the most popular for overseas visitors._

Sixteen in one short conversation! I think you will agree that it is worth using words like _would_, _might_ and _could_ properly.

Other points of grammar

1 You don't always want to use the word _very_ before an adjective. You can use _pretty_ + _adjective_. But you can't use _pretty_ + _adjective_ in all cases. We often use it to persuade someone who might not agree with us, e.g. _Do you really think it's nice to live near a Youth Club? I think it would be pretty noisy._
   You can also use _a bit_ + adjective. But remember that _a bit_ gives a negative idea, so use it with a negative adjective: e.g. _a bit crowded_, _a bit isolated_.

2 Never say 'I am agree'. It is grammatically incorrect. **Always say: _I agree_.**

3 _Whereas_ is a useful word when you are comparing ideas, e.g. _The town's probably going to be the most popular overall, whereas the other two are probably better for one age group._

4 Often you have to make choices in the Part 3 discussion. This is a useful way of expressing them: _So the town would be the most popular, then the village, then the large house and garden._

5 The verb _depend (it depends whether...)_ can be very useful in this sort of coversation. See page 35.

6 Make sure you understand how to use these forms properly: _have you, didn't they, won't we, isn't it_, etc. They are called questions tags and are used a great deal in English conversation to check if the other speaker agrees or understands, or perhaps to help the communication along and encourage the other speaker to join in.

Before you do this last Practice Exercise, look through the *Useful Language* sections for the first two Practice Exercises again.

PRACTICE EXERCISE 3

I'd like you to imagine that you have been asked to plan the food for a birthday party for a 7-year-old girl and 9 of her friends. You can afford to buy something from 5 of the 8 sections in the supermarket that you see in the plan below. You must decide together which 5 sections you will buy from and say why.

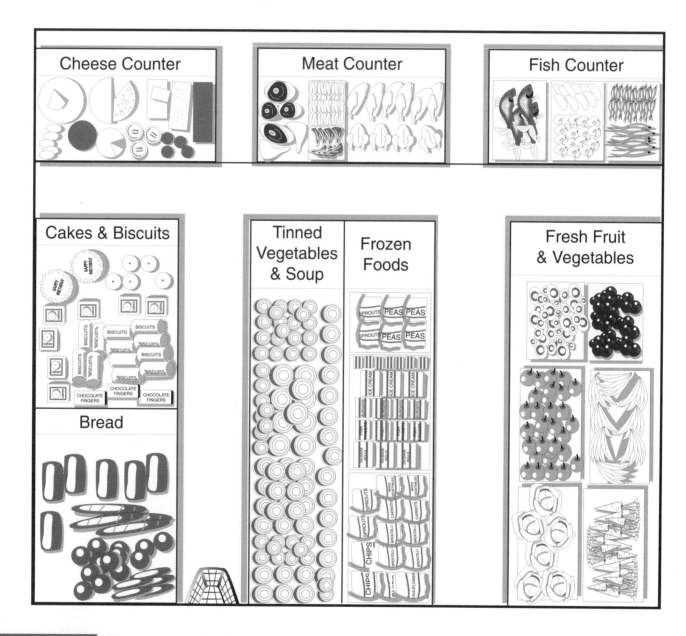

USEFUL LANGUAGE

Focus on content

It may seem to you that the topic you are asked to discuss in the exam is not very interesting and you may feel that you haven't got much to say about it. But the conversation must last for 3 minutes, and if you don't keep it up in a reasonably fluent and thoughtful way, then you will lose marks. So you must be ready to try and find something to say. It's probably a good idea to organise in your head the different sorts of areas that you are asked about and see which ones you can best build on. In Practice Exercise 3 it may seem at first that all you can do is mention five foods and that's it. Let's investigate this a bit further, though.

It says you must plan the food for a birthday party. So you know already that you can discuss the idea that it is a birthday, and that it is a party, which usually has quite special food. If you are planning it, then you also need to talk about how the food will be prepared. Then it says that it is for a 7-year-old girl and her friends. This is another point of discussion – what do little children like to eat? Let me give you an example, in a diagram, of what this part of the discussion could contain. Here I am imagining two British people talking – of course the choices will be different for different nationalities.

Which sections shall we buy from?	Meat	Fish	Bread	Cake	Frozen food
What shall we buy?	chicken	tuna	brown	chocolate	strawberry icecream
How shall we offer it?	hot, fried	cold, with salad	as sandwiches	with icing and birthday candles	in little bowls

This shows you how many different levels there can be in this discussion. All the way through there is likely to be some disagreement, other suggestions made, reasons for choosing or leaving out certain sections and so on. You also have to say why you are choosing certain foods – there could be many reasons for this. When talking about why you have made these choices, you can consider things like:

* what small children like
* how much different foods cost
* how long it takes to prepare the different foods
* how healthy the foods are
* what it is traditional to have at a birthday party.

If you think hard enough and have the confidence to say to yourself that it is possible to achieve the task they set you, then you will be all right even if the topic isn't your favourite.

SELF ASSESSMENT

Think about the Practice Exercises that you have done in this part. Now answer these questions to yourself. Did you:

* listen to the other person's suggestions and opinions and encourage them to speak if necessary?
* make enough suggestions yourself and give good reasons?
* take proper turns in the conversation?
* avoid long silences?
* manage to explain if you forgot a word?
* use words like *would*, *might* and *could* in the right places?
* think about your grammar, pronunciation, vocabulary and fluency?
* complete the task, i.e. come to a decision? (You won't necessarily lose marks if you don't, but you should be working towards agreement when the 3 minutes are finished.)

Exam tip

Make sure you have plenty of conversations in English. But also, listen to conversations in your first language. Consider how communication works in your first language and see if there are any differences in how people take turns, interrupt each other, encourage the other speaker, agree and disagree with each other, and so on. This exercise will help you focus on what you have been practising in this part.

LOOKING AT PART 4

In Part 4 the interlocutor leads a discussion between you and another candidate. Remember that although the interlocutor takes part in the discussion, he or she will expect the candidates to do as much of the talking as possible. The discussion will take 4 minutes. The main point about Part 4 is that the discussion will be about a topic connected to the task you did in Part 3. You will see what this means when you do the three Practice Exercises. They are all based on the Practice Exercises in Part 3, just as they are in the exam.

WHAT'S BEING TESTED

The assessor will be listening to see how good all your spoken language skills are – including grammar, pronunciation, vocabulary and fluency – but what is especially important in this part is how well you
- exchange information with the other speakers
- give your opinions
- offer good reasons for your opinions.
As in Part 3, you must also show that you can
- agree and disagree in good English
- encourage the other candidate to join in the discussion.
You will also gain marks if you
- start new topics appropriately
- develop subjects that have been introduced.

DOING THE EXAM

Here are some hints for you to think about, to help you with Part 4 of the Speaking Paper.
Try to
- make the discussion flow, offering a new thought if there is a break
- give reasons for what you say, and give examples if you can
- say *I think so* or *I don't think so*, (not: 'I think yes' or 'I think no')
- ask the other speaker what he or she thinks.

Try not to dominate the conversation – the other candidate must join in as much as you – but don't be shy either.
Try not to mumble – it's important to speak clearly even when you haven't had much time to work out what you are going to say.
Try not to worry if you completely disagree with the other person – as long as you say firmly and politely what your opinions are in good English, this is what the assessor is looking for.

PRACTICE EXERCISES

If you can find one or two people to discuss the topics in the Practice Exercises with, answering the questions in each one, this will give you genuine practice for this last part.

As before, I suggest you record it, if possible, listen carefully to your first conversation and then look at the relevant *Useful Language* section. Have the conversation again after that if you possibly can.

Don't forget that the discussion should take about 4 minutes.

PRACTICE
EXERCISE 1

In this Practice Exercise the emphasis is on putting forward arguments, that is, giving your opinion about something and then giving an objective reason – that is, a reason that isn't just a personal thought: it might be a fact about animals or conditions in zoos that you have seen, or an idea that you think is important about what is a right or wrong thing to do. You will notice that the word *should* appears in most of the questions. This is a strong indication that you are being asked to give your thoughtful opinion about some difficult general matters.

Here are the questions

- Are you in favour of zoos and wildlife centres? What are the arguments for and against them?

- What kind of animals should be kept in zoos? Why?

- Do you think animals should have any basic rights? What should they be? Why?

- Do you have a pet? Should anyone be allowed to keep any kind of animal as a pet?

- Should people be allowed to keep dangerous dogs?

USEFUL
LANGUAGE

All three *Useful Language* sections in this part build on the ones in earlier parts. So it would be a good idea to look back at those first to remind yourself of the language of agreeing, disagreeing, asking for the other speaker's opinion and so on, before you repeat this exercise or go on to the next two.

I have underlined some of the important words and expressions.

Putting forward an argument

Make a statement, e.g.:
- *Children can learn what animals look like when they visit a zoo, <u>so I support</u> them.*
- *Animals that are dying out should be in zoos, <u>to save</u> them from extinction.*
- *The condidtions in a Wildlife Park are <u>much better than</u> in a zoo.*
- *Animals <u>should</u> be allowed their freedom.*
- *Anyone <u>should</u> be allowed a pet <u>as long as</u> they look after them.*
- *You have to <u>draw the line somewhere</u> – wild animals shouldn't be pets.*
- *<u>It's up to you</u> what pet you keep.*

Emphasising your point:
- *I <u>feel very strongly</u> about this.*
- *<u>The point is</u> the animals have much more space in a Park.*
- *<u>You see</u>, cats and dogs have been domestic for thousands of years.*
- *Keeping a lion <u>would certainly</u> be unnnatural.*
- *To keep a dog, deliberately, knowing it's dangerous, is <u>totally</u> wrong.*
- *Knowing they will attack human beings is <u>absolutely</u> dreadful.*
- *I <u>do</u> feel that zoos are often cruel.*

When you get stuck (that is, you don't understand or can't think of the right word in English):
- *I've forgotten what a wildlife park is.*
- *What does "deliberately" mean?*
- *I can't think of the right word. It's a sort of ......(use different words to explain)*

Exam tip

You could practise using these expressions talking to yourself from time to time!

PRACTICE EXERCISE 2

In this Practice Exercise the questions for discussion are generally more personal. You still have to give your opinion about things, but this time you are also giving some personal information about where you live, shop, go on holiday and so on. You will then need to suggest what the advantages and disadvantages of some of these are. So you must think about giving your personal views, and reasons both for and against different ways of doing things. You will find one general question at the end, more like the questions in Practice Exercise 1.

Here are the questions

- Do you live in the town or country? What are the advantages and disadvantages of where you live?

- If you were to live in a different country, which would you choose? Why?

- Do you go away for holidays sometimes? Where? What do you like doing?

- What would your dream holiday be? Why?

- Do you think local residents always welcome tourists? What effect can they have on the people and the area?

USEFUL LANGUAGE

Here are some examples of different things you could say in this discussion. They don't form a conversation themselves but are some ideas for you to study and adapt to what you would like to say. They are a mixture of personal information, opinions and reasons for and against. As before, I have underlined some of the useful words and expressions.

- *One advantage is that we're close to London. It's quite peaceful here and everyone knows each other. But then it takes over half an hour to get to the shops. Another disadvantage is the amount of petrol we have to use. From my father's point of view, it's not that (i.e. very) easy travelling to work.*

- *I live in a block of flats 28 storeys high on an estate, on the east of Hong Kong island. Getting to the flat from work is difficult because there's so much pollution. But against that, the atmosphere is lovely and you can walk around at night without thinking twice about it (i.e. without worrying about crime).*

- *It has to be the South of France! Because of the attitude of the people, the quality of the food, the space and the climate.*

- *I like swimming, sightseeing, relaxing, taking it easy, visiting temples, going to markets, camping, bird-watching, taking photographs, eating out, sailing, fishing, walking, riding, climbing, sunbathing, shopping.*

- *For me it would probably be Bali – my mother's told me how peaceful and beautiful it is there, but I probably wouldn't want to come home!*

- *I'd very much like to go to Beijing, but my dream holiday would be to go to ... the Grand Canyon in the United States.*

- *People in the county of Cornwall like the money the tourists bring in but I don't think they actually like the people, because they drop litter and things.*

- *Tourism means that the environment is spoilt for the people living there, doesn't it?*

- *The problem with tourism is that it brings money in but that money doesn't necessarily go to those who need it most in the area.*

- *There are lots of examples of local poor people not benefiting – you know, busloads of people come to see them and take photos of them, and the tour operators charge a lot of money, but the local people don't see much of that money.*

- *Tourists certainly should be stopped from going to certain places – for example in Egypt, they've had to close some of the tombs at the Valley of the Kings to save the paintings from the light and air. The same thing applies to many old churches and cave paintings. Sometimes the money that tourism brings helps keep something going, but at the same time helps to destroy it.*

- *So tourism is important but it needs to be controlled.*

In this last Practice Exercise, try to think about all the different aspects of language that you have practised so far for the Speaking Paper. As well as that, you should now try hard to say more than one or two sentences at a time. In other words, try and develop the topic in an interesting way. You will find some examples of this in the *Useful Language* section.

PRACTICE EXERCISE 3

Here are the questions

- Are you good at cooking? What can you make?

- Describe a typical food shopping morning for someone in your country.

- Do you like your country's food? Why?/Why not?

- Is there another country's food you know? What is it like?

- What kind of parties do you like? Why?

Developing the topic

USEFUL LANGUAGE

Although you don't need to learn all of the vocabulary I'm giving you here (some of the words in this list are above First Certificate level), you might find it very useful to be familiar with some of the words if you are asked about food in the exam. For example, you might want to use some of the following:

- Fruits: *apples, oranges, bananas, apricots, plums, cherries, melon, coconuts, currants*
- Vegetables: *lettuce, tomatoes, cabbage, carrots, beans, peas, onions, garlic*
- Meat: *pork, beef, lamb, chicken, pigeon, bacon, ham*
- Fish: *salmon, trout, herring, shellfish (like shrimps, prawns, crabs), cod, carp*
- Other foods: *cheese, bread, eggs, pasta, yogurt, nuts, butter, jam, salt, pepper, spices*
- Dishes: *soup, stew, curry, puddings, sauce*
- Steps in cooking: *cut, chop, mix, peel, stir, turn over*
- Methods of cooking: *bake, fry, roast, boil, grill, smoke*

Here are some examples of responses to some of the questions in Practice Exercise 3. They are a little longer than other examples I've given you. This is to give you an idea of developing the topic a bit further than one sentence. You'll see that you don't need to speak in such an organised way as you would write, but the ideas should be connected and make sense.

- *In Hong Kong it's usual for people to shop twice a day, once in the morning to buy fresh food for lunch and once in the afternoon for the evening meal. For example chickens would be killed on the spot and taken home, cooked and eaten within an hour of being killed. There are also specialist shops for food like dried fish or meat, pressed duck for instance, which is dried in the wind. Shopping there is really exciting, and one can have western food too – supermarkets stock most of the things you'd find in an American supermarket, now.*

- *Where I live, in England, I always go to my supermarket, but there are markets too where you can get cheese and clothes and lots of different things for the house, plants too. In the supermarket, you can get more or less everything you want, just fill up your trolley from the shelves as you walk up and down, and then pay for it all at the end – at the check out. You have to have a car, though, for that kind of shopping, and most people in Britain do.*

- *French food is something I enjoy very much. The French always use fresh ingredients, and they take great care with their food and how they cook it – they always like to cook well for their families. It's not only very fresh, but often very simple too. It's full of interesting things and is quite delicious. I particularly like their breakfast bread rolls and coffee. They certainly know how to make good sauces too.*

- **A**: *I like discos, because I like loud music, and good dancing.*
  B: *I don't agree at all – I can't bear discos – I like to go to parties to talk to people, meet interesting new people and really talk to them.*
  A: *But you can dance **and** talk at discos.*
  B: *Well, I don't think so I'm afraid – I used to like dancing but I don't any more...*
  A: *I like the sort of party where you get an invitation and you can invite your own friends as well so everyone comes along!*
  B: *I find that a rather difficult idea because firstly it could mean that too many people come and secondly they might not be the sort of people you want.*

(You could try and continue this conversation in your head or with someone else!)

SELF ASSESSMENT

Think about the Practice Exercise that you have just done. Now answer these questions to yourself.
Did you follow some of the advice I gave to you earlier? In particular, did you:

- think of plenty of ideas to put forward?
- go on for four minutes without long silences?
- say enough to develop the topic properly from time to time?
- mention both advantages and disadvantages where suitable?
- emphasise your point using suitable English?
- get out of any problem you had (e.g. not knowing a word you needed)?

Exam tip

- Smile, look friendly and appear confident.
- Follow the advice I have given you for the Speaking Paper, especially about taking turns in your conversation, listening to what the other speakers say and picking up on their ideas in your own responses.

Answers,
Notes
and
Tapescripts

You will find that in different exercises the notes I have given to help you are presented in different ways, sometimes with the answers, sometimes with the tapescript. This is to make them as easy as possible to use in each case, and as helpful.

Parts of the tapescripts that are underlined contain the main clues to the answers. Where there is a number, this refers to the number of the question.

2 Listening Part 1: Multiple Choice

PRACTICE EXERCISE 1

ANSWERS

1 *Who?*   Someone wanting to let or sell a flat
  Where? In a flat
2 *Who?*   Swimming student and teacher
  Where? In the water
3 *Who?*   Police Officer and car driver
  Where? In the road
4 *Who?*   Business colleagues
  Where? At the airport
5 *Who?*   Employer interviewing someone for a job
  Where? In a room used for job interviews

To answer the question: *How do you know?* look at the keywords which are underlined for you in the tapescript and the notes.

TAPESCRIPT AND NOTES

Question 1
And finally, the <u>kitchen</u>, with a wonderful <u>view</u> even though it's small... well, that's it. Shall we go down <u>in the lift</u> as we're on the 8th floor here, and you can <u>tell me if you're interested</u>? (**Note:** this suggests that the speaker wants to know if the other person is interested in the flat. Also it's likely to be a flat as most houses don't have eight floors)

Question 2
A: I can't seem to get the <u>legs</u> right – they keep <u>going down</u>, and the rest of me with them.
B: Let's try it again with <u>my hand supporting you</u> – don't worry, you won't <u>drown</u>!

Question 3
A: Bit of damage to your roof and side window there...
B: Yes, <u>Officer</u>, you see... (**Note:** this is how to address a Police Officer)
A: May I see your <u>licence</u> please? (**Note:** it must be a driving licence as roof and side window have been mentioned)
B: I'm afraid I haven't got it with me.
A: Then I shall have to ask you to bring it to the <u>Police Station</u> within 5 days. (**Note:** this shows that it is certain to be a Police Officer speaking)

Question 4
A: Ms Stanley? (**Note:** a formal way of greeting, so they can't be close friends)
B: Oh hello, you must be Mr Chance. Let me help you with <u>that bag</u>. I hope you had a <u>good journey</u>.
A: Well, it wasn't very smooth <u>in those clouds up there</u>, but we're still in time for the <u>meeting</u>, aren't we? (**Note:** a flight is the only kind of journey in the clouds up there).

Question 5

I see from <u>your application form</u> that you are <u>highly qualified</u> and speak two other languages – that's something we see as an <u>essential skill</u>. How would you see them as being <u>useful</u> in this context? (**Note:** the underlined words all suggest a job interview)

Speaker no. 2 is expressing an opinion about a film

Keywords: <u>incredible</u> + <u>job</u> (**Note:** this suggests a positive reaction like admiration)

<u>with Emma Thompson in</u>, <u>screenplay</u> (**Note:** in English, actors star **in** a film – characters can be **in** a book too, but only a film has screenplay)

Speaker no. 1 is receiving directions to the hairdresser

Keywords: <u>which shopfront</u>, <u>beyond there</u>, <u>get...hair cut</u>

Speaker no. 5 is apologising for braking suddenly

Keywords: <u>didn't know you were so close behind me</u> (**Note:** this suggests that he wouldn't have stopped suddenly if he'd seen the person behind)

<u>forgive me</u> (**Note:** this is quite a strong apology in English)

Speaker no. 3 is reporting on a plane crash

Keywords: <u>trail of smoke</u>, <u>downwards out of control</u>, <u>pilot</u>

<u>This is Tim Rees, Aberdeen</u> (**Note:** this is a standard type of ending to a news bulletin)

Speaker 4 is describing a photograph

Keywords: <u>beautiful</u>

<u>come out as</u> (**Note:** e.g. 'This photo has come out well/badly')

Speaker 1

A: I'm sorry I don't see... <u>which shopfront</u> do you mean? Oh, no, I see – that bright blue one – just <u>beyond there</u>, you say?

B: That's it – you'll <u>get your hair cut</u> there.

Speaker 2

It's that one <u>with Emma Thompson in</u> – in fact I think she wrote the <u>screenplay</u> too, an <u>incredible job</u> she made of it too.

Speaker 3

All I could see against the setting sun was a distant flame in the air with a <u>trail of smoke</u> disappearing <u>downwards out of control</u>, it seemed. I only heard later that the <u>pilot</u> had escaped safely. <u>This is Tim Rees, Aberdeen</u>.

Speaker 4

Here's Lake Victoria – <u>beautiful</u> isn't it? But I'm afraid the elephant under the tree there has only <u>come out as</u> a tiny dot.

Speaker 5

There were these two chickens just marching across the road, so I had no choice – I <u>didn't know you were so close behind me</u> – please <u>forgive me</u>, I do hope you're all right.

1 No. (**Note:** the word <u>envelopes</u> suggests that this must refer to first and second class stamps.)

2 No. (**Note:** the word <u>ridiculous</u> is quite a long way from the beginning of the sentence but it means that he thinks the new road is a silly idea.)

3 Maybe. (**Note:** although the blood tests didn't show an infection – <u>were negative</u> – it doesn't prove anything. It's possible she may have one. Note that the words <u>It's true that</u>... are often followed by <u>but</u>...)

4 Yes. (**Note:** she does agree, in this case, but implies that the customer normally needs a receipt.)

5 Yes. (**Note:** <u>other than</u> means except. So he wants hand guns forbidden everywhere except in shooting clubs. This means keeping them in shooting clubs is all right, but not in private homes.)

Question 1

Twenty for this country and five for Greece please... I'll stick those onto the <u>envelopes</u> now... yes, his wife's brother-in-law won the top prize! Oh, I've got no change I'm afraid... he had to share it with eight others, but still...

Question 2

The idea that this new road is going to make a large difference to the town's population, making their lives easier by taking a lot of traffic away, is <u>ridiculous</u>.

Question 3

I'm not saying I'm certain yet. <u>It's true that</u> both the blood tests we have taken have been negative, <u>but</u> this doesn't mean you haven't got an infection.

Question 4

A: I'm afraid my receipt got thrown out. I've only got this document here from my bank showing the date and the amount I paid your company.

B: It's not a receipt, is it?

A: No, but...

B: I'll make an exception, but you should really have a receipt.

Question 5

A senior Police Inspector is suggesting that keeping hand guns at home should be made against the law. He says there's no need to keep hand guns <u>other than</u> at shooting clubs. He also supports the idea of psychological testing for those wishing to hold a licence.

This time the keywords are underlined in the tapescript and extra notes are made by each answer:

1 **A** (**Note:** <u>but</u> after <u>bacon sandwiches</u> suggests that he is going to make something else)

2 **A** (**Note:** here it's helpful to have a picture in your mind of someone trying to "manage" a telephone directory, holding it away from them – this image suggests someone having difficulty reading small print.)

3 **C** (**Note:** the wet spell was in the past [<u>It's been</u> ...]. In the phrase <u>most of it</u>..., 'it' refers to sunshine, not to rain. It's the coast which will have rain and frost.)

4 **B** (**Note:** <u>caught</u> on the security camera suggests the man was probably committing an offence [a crime]. The cheque wasn't discovered later. They discovered later that it was a stolen cheque.)

5 **C** (**Note:** together the underlined words all suggest that this must refer to a photograph.)

6 **A** (**Note:** using <u>a</u> with the name Jim Banks suggests that Lindy has never heard of him. <u>There must be</u>... means that someone else [i.e. Kevin] has probably made a mistake, not Lindy. Kevin thinks it's <u>mysterious</u> because he thought this was Jim Banks' number.)

Question 1

I love bacon sandwiches, <u>but</u> omelette's better still – and it's quite easy: first <u>break all the eggs</u> into a bowl and beat them together really well. Slice some bacon, and onions if you want and fry them gently till they are just crisp. Then put the <u>egg mixture</u> into the frying pan and add the bacon. Let it all cook before you fold it over, and then <u>serve with</u> delicious warm brown bread. It goes well with green salad and tomatoes.

Question 2

I'm fine in the bright light and early morning – especially if I've slept well the night before, but by the evening I find I have to <u>hold things a long way from my face</u> and <u>half close my eyes</u>, and I <u>can't manage telephone directories</u> at all!

Question 3

It's been time to get those umbrellas out this week what with all the <u>rain</u> we've had – drying up now, with not too much sunshine this afternoon – most of <u>it</u> in the sheltered west. For tonight in <u>coastal areas</u> some <u>rain</u> and a widespread ground <u>frost</u>.

Question 4

This man was <u>caught</u> on the bank's security cameras. He's five foot eight, in his early to mid 50s. Last Tuesday a bank clerk became <u>suspicious</u> and <u>refused to cash his cheque</u>. The man became angry and left the bank. The cheque was <u>later discovered to have been stolen</u>.

Question 5

Could you get a bit closer together – <u>I can't get you all in</u> – oh do stop moving about, it'll take longer and probably won't be <u>clear and sharp</u>. Look, wait a minute let me get the <u>distance</u> right. OK, ready everyone? <u>Smile!</u>

Question 6

Lindy: 45832. Lindy speaking.
Kevin: Hello, may I speak to Jim please?
Lindy: Jim who?
Kevin: Jim Banks.
Lindy: Who's speaking please?
Kevin: Kevin. Is he there?
Lindy: Hold the line – I'm sorry I can't trace <u>a Jim Banks</u>. <u>There must be some mistake</u>.
Kevin: How mysterious.

1 A
2 A
3 C
4 B
5 B
6 A
7 C
8 B

Question 1

Woman: Do you think the skirt's all right – does it hang properly? I don't want the guests thinking it's not straight...

Man: The guests? There's only one guest you've got to worry about, I'd say! <u>I wouldn't be surprised if you were next!</u> But it looks very nice, and that colour suits you very well. You'll look wonderful.

Woman: Shall I decide on this one then – are you sure? I think it's quite a reasonable price, don't you?

Man: I'm sure – and I think the <u>bride and bridegroom</u> will like it too.

Question 2

It's the largest one in the entire <u>African continent</u> and its size, brown head, neck and underparts distinguish it from all the others, which are smaller and differently coloured. When young, it's paler and has a greyish-white <u>tail</u>. From a distance you can recognise it by its yellow <u>beak</u> which it's really quite easy to see. It lives both away from the shore and on coastal waters – and is common <u>on</u> Lake Baringo in Kenya, where it <u>nests</u> in a colony on Gibraltar Island.

Question 3

....they can <u>sense when their owner's coming back</u>, if they've been away. They're very sensitive and when <u>you can't see anything</u> that could have caught your dog's attention, they'll stare with <u>their fur standing up on the back of their neck, as if there's a spirit of the dead, and growl</u>, like they do before an earthquake. We see them as very male animals whereas other animals are different. Rabbits represent fear for instance, and cats are associated with scary things like black magic – and they don't do things like <u>bark</u> at the moon.

Question 4

This week the team are all over the world. I'm at the Chelsea Show admiring the most glorious roses which bring back happy memories of <u>plant-hunting</u> in the heat of Greece, round the Temple of Apollo. Isobel's in Crete looking at some beautiful <u>wild flowers</u> related to a very common <u>garden type</u>, Alan's in Turkey hoping to find out the connection between special flowers and oriental hats, while Liz is enjoying the scents and sights of Italian <u>vegetables</u>. Mediterranean sunshine and English showers provide the contrasts in this week's programme.

Question 5

Boy:	So are you broke now?
Girl:	Yeah, almost, though no, we stayed somewhere owned by the Irish Students Union in the old part, so it was quite cheap...
Boy:	How did you get about then, without spending a fortune?
Girl:	Well, there's this double decker sightseeing bus – only been going about a month – and for about £6.00, I think it was, it'll take you anywhere in the city and drop you off.
Boy:	And where did *you* go?
Girl:	Well we sat and heard about the Duke of Wellington, cathedrals and other more modern stuff, then got to <u>the women's prison, now a museum</u>, and had <u>a guided tour by the administrator</u>.
Boy:	They didn't keep you in then?
Girl:	Ha ha very funny.

Question 6

Woman:	Then Smith sent one straight down the middle – brilliant they called it in the newspaper later! – giving Jones an almost impossible task.
Man:	And did Jones manage anything after that?
Woman:	Well, yes actually, amazingly he managed a really skilful shot in reply with a quick flick of <u>his racket</u> and left Smith on his knees in the middle of <u>the court</u> looking as if he was praying for help!
Man:	Did you stay to the end?
Woman:	Oh yes, because it was nail-biting. Finally Jones took the lead, but he suddenly seemed to lose his confidence and <u>his opponent</u> took the opportunity to force some mistakes from Jones and <u>ended up winning</u>.

Question 7

<u>I am obliged</u> to test your breath using a screening instrument known as an SL2 meter. I'd like you to provide me with a sample of your breath. I'd like you to take a deep breath and blow into this tube, strongly enough to light Light A and for long enough to light Light B. If you don't blow hard enough, Light A won't light, and if you don't blow for long enough, we won't have a sufficient amount of sample. I shall tell you when to stop blowing. <u>I must point out to you that failure to provide me with a sample of your breath may make you liable for arrest.</u>

Question 8

Woman: Many people don't care about it these days – it costs the British people a lot, and I don't think we really benefit much – in any case it doesn't really make sense to be part of Europe *and* have a King or Queen.

Man: But remember the world is getting smaller and I think we need them, and we need to know who we are – what we mean to ourselves as a nation – and also Britain needs all the representatives abroad it can get, to help other countries understand us.

Woman: Representatives yes, but professional ones, you know, as part of the government or something, and we'd still know who we are if Britain was a republic like the rest of the world – or most of it anyway.

1 B
2 C
3 C
4 B
5 B
6 A
7 C
8 B

Question 1

Sometimes a bad cold can turn into an illness called flu – spelt F L U. Anyone can catch flu, even the fittest of people. Flu can make you feel ill for several days with a high fever, headache, aching limbs and weak muscles. You may also develop a dry cough, and painful throat and troublesome nose. But the worst part of flu is the risk it brings of other serious illnesses. It is particularly threatening to people with heart disease for example. For this reason the Department of Health recommends that all this group of people should receive an injection against it each year.

TAPESCRIPT

Question 2

Recently I've been checking all deliveries received from BNT Ltd as they seem to have been incomplete. Last Thursday I saw our driver, Michael White, draw his lorry up to the delivery door at the back of the storage room. He unlocked his vehicle and lifted its rear shutter and handed our storage man a delivery note. Together they unloaded the stock from the lorry into a box, all of which which I could see from a hidden area, up some stairs. The storage man then went to the general office and the driver removed two small cardboard boxes from the box and put them into his lorry.

Question 3

It consists of the upper storey of an old house which is just outside the village; it is all on one floor but it's arranged as two separate flats. Although each one has its own entrance, this set-up could well suit two families wishing to go on holiday together. There are magnificent views over the valley at the front, and it's set into a hill with trees behind. There's lots to do: river swimming a few minutes' walk away and the coast is about 8 kilometres to the north. These are cheerful, comfortable properties, furnished with a mixture of old and new in the traditional style.

Question 4

• What's the appeal of jazz to you and tell me why the trumpet?

• It's the feeling – every night you go out and play something, maybe you play the same old tunes, but I try and pick tunes that are good musically, and play them in my own way – and the trumpet, well it chose me really, I always wanted to be a drummer then when I was in the navy there was a trumpet available – well an instrument called the bugle to begin with actually – but I changed later. I picked it up, found I could play a few notes and it took me up, as it were. The bugle only plays about seven or eight notes, but this thing you get millions of notes on. Shall I give you a tune, a *new* one!

Question 5

- So how are things going? Has Diane had it yet?
- Yes, hasn't news reached you? 2.30 in the morning – it took 6 hours but then she had a healthy baby girl. I'm on my way from there now.
- How wonderful, and is she all right, and what about John – a proud father no doubt?
- Oh yes, he's so happy – he said he was over the moon with joy. She's got the most beautifully shaped ears – they must come through the male line – Diane's stick out! <u>She has completely black hair, but apart from that, looks just like her Dad</u> – she's even got his curls!

Question 6

Life on the Queen Mary in the thirties was very luxurious you know. There were six miles of carpets, metres and metres of leather, lounges, music rooms and entertainers – if you travelled first-class, your accommodation included room for your servant, but you know in the heavy Atlantic seas <u>it rolled and funny things happened</u>. I remember on our way back to Southampton <u>there was this piano that got loose and slid round this lounge</u> – no-one could do anything about it. <u>For three days</u> it sounded like a mad unstoppable pianist – absolutely magnificent!

Question 7

- Is this yours?
- No, but the next one in the series is. It's excellent. <u>I couldn't put it down till the last page</u>. I did nothing else for three days – it drove my parents mad!
- Did you like it better than the first one?
- Well I don't know, I <u>only</u> saw the film, <u>so it's hard to compare</u>, but anyway I'd really recommend it – it's about a different island, with different characters. In fact they discover the island and they find these two kids who came out of nowhere, just hiding in a van. I can't remember what happens after that.

Question 8

I love those little fishing boats <u>in the front here</u>, with their oars laid across the bench seats, reflecting the evening sun, and the strip of water behind the boats going round and disappearing out of sight. And the man standing on the shore who has just caught a beautiful fish, so beautifully <u>drawn</u>, hanging in the air almost ready to swing into the fisherman's hand. Through the mist and cloud <u>in the background</u> are the hills I used to explore as a child, you know – I remember taking my dog for a walk there and he would go after rabbits and get lost for hours!

Exam tip

In Part 1 you must be prepared to jump between very different situations. You may hear a jolly little conversation, then something very serious, then something strange, and so on. Therefore the kind of English used will be different too. Your mind must be very active during Part 1.

3 Listening Part 2: Note Taking

In the tapescripts you will find some words underlined with a number written next to them. This means that these words should help you with the answer to that question. As with all the Practice Exercises, a few extra notes are given in the answers. Where there is no extra comment, the underlined words in the tapescripts should give you the help you need.

1 customers with cars
2 town centres change
3 outside town centres (**Note**: <u>there was no question that</u>... means it was certain that...)

And now an item on shopping in Britain. The movement out of the high street by the major supermarkets started in a big way in the 1980s. The 'everything-under-one-roof' idea <u>for a large supermarket</u>, a superstore as it is known, with lots of parking, <u>attracted many car-owning customers</u> (1). <u>But there was a price to pay. Town-centres began to change</u> (2) – in some cases, becoming rather empty in a very short time – as competition from the out-of-town centres changed the face of the traditional high street. <u>By 1994, there was no question that edge-of-town and out-of-town sites were the most popular with the supermarkets for new development</u> (3), with 64% of new stores being built there.

1 to travel (**Note:** it's not just the map that tells us this – the whole conversation is about where they will travel)
2 with their eyes shut/blindfold (**Note:** this is a little game they play in order to pick out somewhere in the world to go to)
3 no (**Note:** the second speaker doesn't like high or steep places and makes the excuse that she will be busy this summer and so won't be able to go)

- What's that?
- <u>A map of the world. Like an invitation, isn't it</u>...
- <u>What a great idea! Want a companion? I'd love to</u>... (1)
- Are you serious?
- Depends where you're planning to go! That page doesn't look very interesting.
- OK, I'll find somewhere more exciting.
- No, I know, <u>let's do this without looking – you go through the pages and stop when I say – and I'll cover my eyes</u> (2) and put my finger anywhere on the page.
- All right, but I'm allowed to change my mind!
- Agreed – ready?
- Here goes.
- Stop! Where's the map? OK. That feels a good place – now let's see our destiny – fantastic – Venezuela, look!
- Mm, looks like we're going to a waterfall – that's the Angel Falls there...
- What? I hate heights... Er...um... <u>on second thoughts, I may be busy this summer – sorry!</u> (3)

PRACTICE EXERCISE 3

ANSWERS AND NOTES

You'll find extra notes with the answers in the next three exercises because you had to say what kind of question each one was, as well as give the answer.

1 By reading (about it)   (Deduction. **Note:** she's clearly reading out the information from a page).

2 3 days and 2 nights   (Detail. **Note:** we could understand the important points of the conversation without knowing the exact length of the holiday)

3 Because his is in poor condition   (Deduction)

4 No   (Deduction. **Note:** it's the luggage which goes by car, not people)

5 Answer some questions   (Main point. **Note:** <u>to enter</u>... etc. means that in order to do the competition, you must answer the questions)

6 Answer the questions/enter the competition   (Deduction. **Note:** Jack's question <u>What are we waiting for</u>? suggests that he wants to get on and enter the competition quickly in order to win the holiday)

TAPESCRIPT

Annie:	Look at this <u>page! It says here that the winner of this competition gets a short break cycling holiday for two.</u> (1)
Jack:	Hey we could go together! But I'm not very good at it though. Is it in Britain or what?
Annie:	Yes, listen: the prize consists of <u>three days cycling and two nights bed and breakfast</u> (2) on a cycle tour in Herefordshire – passing through pretty villages, meadows and river valleys.
Jack:	Sounds beautiful – I love cycling – it's the perfect way to see the countryside – you're just high enough to see over the hedges and just slow enough to take it all in. But <u>I don't think my bike's up to it</u> (3), and I can't afford a new one at the moment.
Annie:	Shush, I haven't finished: <u>it says</u> (1) you don't have to be an expert – these breaks are designed for beginner cyclists and <u>your luggage will be transported by car</u> (4). You hire an 18-speed cycle, and you can go at your own speed, taking time to stop at local tea shops, historic houses and sit by the banks of the River Lugg. <u>To enter the competition, just answer the following questions.</u> (5)
Jack:	<u>What are we waiting for?</u> (6)

PRACTICE EXERCISE 4

ANSWERS AND NOTES

1 they have visitors   (Deduction/summarising. **Note:** the whole text is about what to do when visitors call)

2 check who's there   (Main point)

3 put the chain on   (Main point)

4 check who they are   (Main point)

5 their telephone no.   (Main point)

6 someone in a hurry   (Main point)

Note: Notice that most of these are Main Point questions – ones where you need to pick out the key points and ignore the details that accompanied them. But if you wrote *summarising* instead of main point, then you were not really wrong – there is a bit of both in these questions.

TAPESCRIPT

<u>The whole text</u> (1)

Old people often suffer from doorstep crime. This is usually from thieves so here is some positive action you can take:

1 Before opening, <u>check to see who is at your door</u> (2), either by looking through the hole in your door if you have one, or by looking out of the window.

2 Always <u>put the chain on before you open the door</u> (3) (they don't cost much). But don't keep it on permanently as this could be dangerous in a fire.

3 <u>If you don't know the visitor, ask to see the card with their name and photo on it</u> (4) and check it carefully. Genuine callers won't mind if you close the door to do this.

4 If you are in any doubt about them, ask them to come back later. You can then check their

story by phoning the organisation or company they claim to represent. <u>Don't believe the telephone number on their card</u> (5), it may be the number of a criminal's partner.

5   If you are still not happy, contact your local Police Station or a neighbour or relative.

6   <u>Be careful of anybody who says they are in a hurry</u> (6) – don't let them put pressure on you. Remember, genuine callers will normally make an appointment first and will carry a card with their photograph on it.

1   1.30 - 4.30 p.m.
2   *two of these:* music, acting, art, computer courses
3   second and third in August
4   fully qualified specialists
5   yes
6   £75
7   book four or more courses
8   no
9   win a competition/tournament
10 yes (at shop)

Don't know what to do with your children this summer? Why not send them to Hanford High School Holiday Activities? They are offering specialist courses in a wide variety of sports and activities which run from 9.30 a.m. to 12.30 p.m. and <u>1.30 to 4.30 p.m.</u> (1). Choose from activities like <u>music</u>, racket sports, football, athletics, <u>acting, art or computer courses</u> (2). Or if you prefer, you can select a multi-activity course (which is a more recreational type course including swimming pool activities) in either of <u>the two age groups</u> (5). This course will include all kinds of new exciting activities. For the more adventurous, you might like to join in an outdoor adventure course – special all day courses that run from 9.30 to 4.30 <u>during the second and third weeks of August</u> (3), with sailing, a climbing wall, mountain bike practice and golf. The children are taught climbing, sailing and swimming activities by <u>specialist fully qualified instructors</u> (4). Children must be able to swim 100 metres and be comfortable in water. They will require a packed lunch.

On all courses, children are organised in small and friendly groups which means that they will be able to learn new skills in a safe environment. <u>The age groups as stated on the course details are intended as a guide</u> (5) as to the suitability of a course for your children. All courses cost £30.00 except <u>the outdoor adventure (special all day course) which costs £75.00</u> (6). There are no hidden extras. Interested? Get in touch with Sandy Ross, Director of Courses, at Hanford High School. Don't delay – you wouldn't want to disappoint the kids! <u>Discounts are available for families who book 4 or more courses</u> (7). Please note that <u>no fees can be returned in case of absence</u> (8). Remember that all children attending receive a certificate, with <u>medals and prizes going to competition and tournament winners</u> (9). Full equipment is provided. Children are most welcome to attend morning and afternoon. <u>During the lunch hour</u> there are adults in charge and <u>snacks and drinks are on sale</u> (10) at the shop.

EXAM EXERCISE 2

ANSWERS

1 sweet things
2 as children/in childhood
3 a sweet tooth
4 breast milk is sweet
5 makes people fat/overweight
6 causes heart disease
7 eating more fruit and vegetables
8 telling them
9 bad for you/harmful
10 too many sweet and fatty foods/a junk diet

TAPESCRIPT

Interviewer: <u>What gives us a sweet tooth?</u>

Doctor: <u>Well, experts are divided on why we love sweet and fat-filled foods</u> (1). <u>Some believe it's a result of how we are brought up</u> (2). Most of us associate sweet food with happy occasions, such as ice cream on holiday, and so desire them later on. <u>Others believe that our bodies are made to enjoy sweetness naturally</u> (3). After all, <u>the first food for most of us – breast milk – is very sweet</u> (4). So is fruit, which is also full of vitamins. Foods such as sugar and honey, are easily digested, which is why we're tempted to eat more of them. Others, like fruit, bread and rice are taken in more slowly, and so feel more satisfying.

Interviewer: So, do you think most people should change their diet, and if so, why?

Doctor: Most of us eat too much fat (the sort that's found in foods containing butter, you know, cakes, biscuits and fatty meats) and not enough fruit and vegetables. The government wants us to reduce the amount of fat and saturated fat we eat. <u>Too much of this kind of fat will not only make us all too heavy</u> (5), <u>but also makes heart disease much more likely</u> (6). <u>By not eating enough fruit and vegetables, we also starve our bodies of vitamins A,C and E, all of which help prevent some cancers</u> (7). A recent report by the World Health Organisation estimates that up to 40% of cancers in men and 60 % in women may be caused by a diet that is too high in animal fats and too low in fruit and vegetables. Scientists also believe what we eat in childhood can set the stage for all sorts of illnesses in later years, from tooth decay to heart disease.

Interviewer: But, how can we encourage our families to eat healthily without spending a fortune, feeling hungry or causing battles at mealtimes?

Doctor: The answer is to <u>put some goodness into their meals without them being aware of it</u> (8). Remember that <u>there's no such thing as junk food</u> – you know, burgers, chips, crisps, etc. (9) – only what we call a junk diet. In other words, the foods themselves are not all bad, it's the amount we eat that is the problem. After all, chips contain Vitamin C and burgers are full of iron. Problems only arise <u>when we eat too much of these so-called junk foods too often</u> (10), instead of other lower fat foods.

Exam tip

You're listening out for a variety of answers in Part 2 and they come quite fast, so you must not only think quickly but write quickly when you think you know the answer, and in the right place! Looking to see what kind of answers might be needed, before you start, is very important.

4 Listening Part 3: Matching Speaker to Text

1 C (**Note:** <u>immediately got on with</u> means they liked them from the start. This sentence suggests that the family were invited to use the pool for the rest of the holiday. <u>I felt sick</u> here just means the speaker was very upset about the pool being closed.)

2 B (**Note:** they wrote to complain to the tour company not their insurers)

3 A (**Note:** <u>the insurance company agreed</u>... suggests that the holiday-makers wrote to them and complained)

Speaker 1

There were these amazingly tempting photos of the pool in the holiday leaflet – that decided it really, so off we went for our family holiday in the sun. Well, imagine how we felt when we were told it'd be closed for cleaning during our second week. I felt sick! But everything turned out all right when my brother met this wonderful local family who had a beautiful pool. <u>They immediately got on with the whole family and so we had a really good time!</u>

Speaker 2

Last September we went on holiday near where we'd been the year before. You won't believe this but it's true – we found the waiters swimming fully clothed in the pool <u>and then</u> we saw it being cleaned with far too many chemicals in the water which made us <u>feel sick after our evening swim</u>. We wasted no time in writing to the tour company about it.

Speaker 3

We had a 30-hour delay on our flight to our 2-week holiday, so we missed our connecting flight (after being travel sick most of the way!). We had to stay in a hotel and buy new tickets for our missed connection. <u>Our insurance company agreed we had a genuine complaint and they paid the £60</u> due for the delay, but they wouldn't pay for the hotel and flight expenses.

1 B

2 D (**Note:** <u>cut price</u> means discounts)

3 A (**Note:** in spoken text 2 the discount is much less than half for old age pensioners)

Speaker 1

We welcome customers in wheelchairs and our staff will be pleased to assist. In the theatre there are <u>six spaces available and six seats for accompanying persons are provided</u> – now offered at half-price. This includes rock concerts.

Speaker 2

<u>Cut price tickets are available for</u> full-time students, <u>the unemployed</u> and the over 60s. They are as follows: £14 tickets reduced to £12. £10 tickets reduced to £8. Book two or more concerts and receive first choice of seats.

Speaker 3

<u>Half-price seats for</u> children under 16, <u>older people</u>, wheelchair users and groups of 10 or more people. 10% off school groups of 10 or more. £5 off plus 1 in 10 free. You can enjoy a meal after an afternoon performance, or before the start of an evening show, in the Roof Garden.

PRACTICE EXERCISE 3

ANSWERS AND NOTES

1 C (**Notes:** <u>the bosses do really well</u>: they receive a lot of money; <u>for themselves</u>: this can often sound critical, as it does here (though not always); <u>fell into their lap</u>: this strengthens the idea that the bosses get something for nothing; <u>I really wonder what they do for it</u>: the speaker is agreeing by suggesting that the bosses probably don't do enough work to deserve so much money)

2 A (**Notes:** <u>Some say</u>: this suggest that the speaker may not agree with what these people say; <u>I don't think...</u>: the word "I" contrasts with "Some" in the first sentence, indicating that "I" will have a different opinion from some people)

3 D (**Note:** the whole message tries to persuade the listener by explaining the steps simply and reminding the listener that it's fun and they might win)

TAPESCRIPT

Number 1

- You know this lottery business – it was all in the news recently...
- <u>Those bosses do really well for themselves</u> don't they, but I suppose other organisations have benefited too. I mean, some of the money does go to the arts and sports I suppose.
- Yes, but it's like winning every week for the bosses! I mean <u>without even buying a ticket on Saturdays, huge amounts fall into their lap</u>, like autumn leaves.
- Yes, and <u>I really wonder what they do for it</u>.

Number 2

<u>Some say</u> it has created a nation of people who can't resist playing the lottery and that it is the poorest who pay out most and that it's socially unfair; <u>also</u> they claim that large amounts of lottery money go to undeserving people instead of to the National Health Service or Cancer Research. <u>I don't think that's a very sensible view – I prefer to regard it as a harmless game which at the same time has its uses</u>.

Number 3

<u>It's easy</u> – you just go down to your local store any time during the week, before Saturday, buy a lottery card, choose six numbers between 1 and 49, mark the card, pay your pound and hand it in. <u>I'm sure you wouldn't regret it – ask anyone . It's good fun and don't forget what they say: the winner could be YOU! Do you want me to come with you?</u>

EXAM EXERCISE 1

ANSWERS

Speaker 1: F
Speaker 2: B
Speaker 3: E
Speaker 4: A
Speaker 5: C

TAPESCRIPT

Speaker 1

This is a beautiful home here, look. It's in a good situation on the London Road. To the front of this property you've got a nicely designed garden, with wonderfully green grass and pretty flowers on both sides <u>enclosed by a good-size fence</u>. You've got a garage with a metal up-and-over door and <u>a secure gate by the road</u>. In the town you'll find a good range of shops and schools – they go up to 18 years old, and there are also <u>playgroups and other services on offer for children who haven't started school yet</u> and a small <u>recreational park contains swings and a roundabout</u>. The other thing you might be interested in is a new Chinese takeaway restaurant and a traditional fish-and-chip shop.

Speaker 2

This home here has three bedrooms and is on its own down a quiet little side street. It's in the popular village of Donley, which you may have driven through, within approximately three quarters of a mile of the local shops, including greengrocers, bakers, butchers, ironmongers, chemists and newsagents. Right behind it is <u>the village sportsground and attractive clubhouse. It</u>

also has a big flat garden about 90 metres long – all grass at the moment, with a lovely brick wall round it. There are two basic pubs down the road, a church and a secondary school. The local bus services are pretty reliable and frequent.

Speaker 3
I think you should have a good look at this house. Here's a picture of it – you see that the accommodation gives a lot of space, with an open-plan split-level lounge, small dining area and, kitchen/breakfast room, four bedrooms and two bathrooms. There's a nice little garden which faces south and has trees, a fishpond and a patio area. There's a one-and-a-half length garage. A lovely little market town this one too, and a great place to dine out, with some fashionable pubs, different nationality restaurants, one of them overlooking the river – a delight in summer – a computer centre, schools and an indoor sports centre.

Speaker 4
Now, this house is only about half a mile up from the village green. It's got an open fireplace, which I always think is lovely – I don't know about you – a modern kitchen, wardrobes and new windows everywhere. A new central heating system has just been put in, and the previous owners extended the garage to make it a double one. They used it as a games room for their children I think. The wide area in front of the house would be suitable for further parking. The town has a secondary school and a basic range of shops including Post Office, butcher, baker, newsagent, petrol station and bank. You can find more in the two neighbouring towns, where there are mainline stations with trains to cities in Wales and Scotland.

Speaker 5
We've got a small but very attractive flat here, in an old building – dating from about 1840. The property has many original features including the windows and doors. It's easy to run in spite of its age because of many modern additions. The rooms are all beautifully painted, and there is someone who would like to continue working in this property keeping it clean and tidy, and also looking after it when there is no-one there, if that is what the new owners wish. There is a parking space in the road for each flat. The town has an outdoor swimming pool. There's a mainline railway station with a regular service to several cities, including the capital. Here you're not far either from two major motorways, which provide a real choice of travel.

Speaker 1: E
Speaker 2: C
Speaker 3: F
Speaker 4: A
Speaker 5: D

EXAM EXERCISE 2
ANSWERS

TAPESCRIPT

Speaker 1
I like meeting customers and making sure they're happy with what I have to offer. It can be an expensive business if you make a mistake – both for the customer and me, I mean, if they go away feeling "I wish it was curly " or "I wish it was straight" they probably won't come back again, even if I offered them a completely different style – for free. I cut for both men and women, and have good conversations with both, but it's irritating if they don't sit still! I find they're both interested in trying out new colours and things, and I always try and guess whether children will ask for the latest fashion!

Speaker 2
I like working with customers who have no idea what they want – that may sound strange but I enjoy starting from the beginning, thinking what style and length would suit them best, giving advice and discussing what they'd like, and then giving them a really good style that shows off their best features and fits them well. I also consider all sorts of other things, like the weather! After all, it's no good looking wonderfully tropical with large patterns of flowers on your clothes if

there's snow on the ground or choosing something warm and wintry if it's likely to be hot. They wouldn't thank me for that. Last week a customer told me I'd made her feel pretty as a picture!

Speaker 3

I don't know really – I think I'm a bit of an artist underneath – I love to experiment with different designs, shapes and colours – it's amazing what you can do with a bit of imagination you know with paths and ponds as well as different flowers. In my job you always have to balance growing with cutting back. When I'm asked to advise on a particular area, I always spend quite a bit of time thinking about it first – you have to think about so many things – what do they want? do they want me to plant vegetables? if yes, summer ones or winter ones? And then there's the weather: if it's a windy place you can't have tropical flowers, for example, and the customers themselves – will they be able to manage after I've finished? Some are willing to do quite a lot, others want it to go on looking good without any further work.

Speaker 4

I find it very satisfying to know that customers are enjoying something that I've created myself – even though I don't always meet them. But word usually gets back to me through the dining room staff serving them. I like the planning part of the job, deciding what to put into each dish and what order to present them in. There's real style in that. There's a lot of skill too, because anyone can do wonderful things with unlimited money, but you've got to think about the cost – something like strawberries or tomatoes are rather expensive in winter for instance in Britain, so you must think about the seasons as well as the end result. What I make may not last long, but the effect and the memory do!

Speaker 5

I always find myself hoping that my work will last – actually sometimes it doesn't because I give up halfway through, throw it away and have to start again with clean brushes. But sometimes things go so well that I'll complete something in a couple of hours. If a particular customer is sitting for me, it can take a long time, especially if we get into a really interesting conversation – then I sometimes make a mistake and mix the wrong colours or something silly and have to go over part of it again, and ask the customer to start sitting still again. Other times, I don't even meet the people who buy my work.

Exam tip

There's always something similar betwen the texts in Part 3. You must look for the differences. Tell yourself you won't get confused. If you keep calm and move your mind on with the tape, you'll be all right. Remember that you hear them all through once first in the exam, and then all of them a second time.

5 Listening Part 4: Multiple Choice or True/False

1 O

2 M (**Note:** Mike had been rescued in a climbing area and it was foggy – this suggests he had had an accident)

3 H (**Note:** she clearly contacted the Police headquarters as a joke and was happy and cheerful about it)

Ann: But I haven't understood why the Police were there?

Tom: Well, as I say, there was this group of tourists in the restaurant – they were celebrating the last evening of their climbing holiday – poor things, they'd had terrible weather and hadn't been able to do much climbing, but they'd had a good time – anyway <u>the Policeman came to see the restaurant owner</u> (1) about <u>a climber called Mike who'd been rescued in the fog</u> (2), and while he was inside, one of the group, Helen, happened to go out and saw the Police car door open. She thought it would be funny to get in, and within a minute or two <u>she was cheerfully talking to the Police headquarters on their radio</u> (3)! You can imagine what the Police Officer felt when he came out of the restaurant and found her!

PRACTICE EXERCISE 1

ANSWERS AND NOTES

TAPESCRIPT

1 M (**Note:** <u>Don't tell me</u> is an idiom meaning you don't need to tell me, I've guessed. Chris was probably going to say, <u>how did you know</u>?)

2 C (**Note:** Chris is frightened the farmer will kill his dog)

3 D (**Note:** Dad is offering to tell the farmer, (<u>I will [tell him] if you like</u>) although he thinks Chris probably should as Benji is his dog)

Mum: Did you enjoy your walk both of you? What's the matter? You look terrible, Chris! Do you feel OK?

Chris: No, an awful thing's happened – you tell her, Dad...

Dad: It's Benji – he was running about quite happily when he saw these sheep...

Mum: In the field you mean?

Dad: Well, no, they were loose, on the road.

Mum: <u>Don't tell me, he attacked them I suppose!</u>

Chris: <u>Yes, how did you ....?</u> (1)

Mum: I've seen him near sheep before and thought he wanted to chase them.

Dad: Well, then he ran after one of them until it fell in the pond and drowned...

Chris: Poor thing, it looked so frightened!

Mum: Oh no, why didn't you keep him on a lead? The farmer will be very angry.

Chris: I know... and <u>I'm scared he'll shoot poor Benji.</u> (2)

Dad: But Mum is right, <u>so someone will have to tell him – I will if you like</u> (3), but he's your dog, Chris.

PRACTICE EXERCISE 2

ANSWERS AND NOTES

TAPESCRIPT

Answers, Notes and Tapescripts

PRACTICE EXERCISE 3

ANSWERS AND NOTES

1 A (**Note:** Andy has clearly spent a lot of money on a good piece of meat because he feels bad that he is going out when it is his turn to cook.)

2 D (**Note:** Dave is clearly keen to get his tickets and Andy's words also suggest that this Rock Concert is very important to Dave.)

3 J (**Note:** Jane doesn't want to cook meat because she's a vegetarian so she doesn't eat meat.)

TAPESCRIPT

Andy: Who's making supper tonight?

Jane: You I hope – it's about time, Andy!

Andy: <u>I know, but the trouble is I'm going out – in fact I'm going to meet my girlfriend's parents, so anyway, I dropped into the butcher's and got you a leg of lamb – here you are</u> (1).

Jane and Dave: Wow!!

Jane: Mmm – that must have cost you a bit, Andy! Pity I don't eat meat – typical! The <u>one time you spend good money on the rest of us</u> (1) I can't join in...

Dave: Ah poor Jane, won't stop the rest of us enjoying it though. Now look , I'm trying to get this finished. <u>If I don't get this application off, I won't get tickets for...</u>

Andy: <u>The Rock Concert! We know! Your favourite band, Yes, yes, Dave... You can't miss that</u> (2)! Well, I'm afraid it must be your turn to cook, Jane, if I'm going out and Dave's busy...

Jane: <u>Me?? Cook something I'm not even going to eat? You must be joking!</u> (3)

PRACTICE EXERCISE 4

ANSWER AND NOTE

A (**Note:** all the words underlined suggest that it must be a photo. In particular <u>it was taken</u>, because in English you *take* a photo, but *write* a diary or a letter.)

TAPESCRIPT

Gail: Give that back – it's private!

David: Don't worry, I won't tell anyone!

Gail: Why should I let you look at it?

David: Well, if you really don't want me to I won't, but I'll go away thinking you've got something nasty to hide... and in any case you're about to send it off, aren't you?

Gail: Oh, all right, but you won't find it very exciting...

David: Looks as if <u>it was taken</u> on holiday – just a minute, I can't quite make this out – what does that say: No swimming!

Gail: So?

David: <u>And there you are, in your swimming costume about to plunge in! And with who, I wonder? Is that the famous Nico perhaps, next to you?</u> Here you are – a stamp for the envelope – <u>he'll probably frame it!</u>

PRACTICE EXERCISE 5

ANSWERS AND NOTES

1 False (**Note:** Sarah was so frightened that she couldn't move – <u>froze</u> has nothing to do with being cold in this sentence.)

2 False (**Note:** the idea of the goose was not the mother's but the Air Force officials' suggestion.)

3 True

Note: In English we call something strange in the sky that no-one can explain an *unidentified flying object* or a *UFO*.

We saw this circle of red lights in the sky. I didn't have a clue what they were but I stopped the car to get a better look. Then Belinda shouted "It's coming this way." We all three sat totally amazed. There were about 10 to 20 red lights standing vertically in the sky like a big clockface, coming towards us slowly. Eventually it was directly above us. If I'd stood on the roof of my car, I could have touched it. Suddenly everything went dark as if a big cloud was passing over – Sarah froze <u>with fear</u> (1). I know it sounds silly but we had to get away – I couldn't let something that threatening come so close to my children. As we drove off, Luke looked back and saw it moving away. We reported what we'd seen to the Royal Air Force and <u>the investigators asked me if I'd seen a goose</u> (2)! I told them if it was, it was the biggest goose I'd ever seen! Since then <u>we've received a standard letter, saying,</u> you know, we don't know what happened, but since <u>it isn't a threat to the country's safety</u> (3), we don't want to investigate any further – usual stuff.

1 True   (**Note:** <u>None</u> means nobody)
2 False   (**Note:** it is the body of the plane that is still there, not a person)
3 True   (**Note:** the words <u>have slipped</u> suggest that parts of the engine fell into the lake after the crash)

Man: It happened on the 13th of June 1945 on a Scottish mountain side. The plane was on its way from Europe, carrying 15 Americans on their way back to the United States. All except one were between 20 and 25. <u>None lived to tell the story</u> (1). You can still see <u>part of the plane's engine and body</u> (2), over 50 years later. <u>Some parts have slipped into the lake nearby</u> (3), other parts are under and round a huge rock where it hit the ground. There's a little plaque with all the names written on.

Boy: I'd like to go there sometime – it sounds a sad but interesting place – a piece of real history.

Man: Yes, I'll take you – it's quite a long walk, up the mountain, but a pretty one on a nice day, and you look pretty fit!

1	L	**5**	B
2	B	**6**	A
3	L	**7**	A
4	A		

Liz: Coffee?

Bob: Thanks. So you're pleased with your new computer are you – not regretting it yet? You used to be rather against too much technology I seem to remember.

Liz: <u>Well, er, I know, but in fact I've become quite a fan, I'm not sure how to tell you this, but, er, um,</u> (1) I've decided to go on the Internet...

Bob: <u>What?? You?? Why? I thought</u> (2) you hated all that stuff and just liked travelling the world and going back to nature and getting to know people!

Liz: Ah, yes, I mean no, look, you see with this, you can actually talk to people on the ground and get grassroots information about what's going on.

Bob: How do you mean – talk to people? It's a machine for goodness' sake!

Liz: So is a telephone, but you don't shout at me for having one of those...You see what I mean is talk as in *communicate* on the net – type in your messages, and the answers come flying back – come on, you could do it too you know – the great thing is that <u>if you travel on your own</u> (3), and you want to find out what's happening on a particular frontier or if there's an outbreak of plague, then <u>you can chat with someone who's just been there and find out – that's what I intend to do for my trip next week.</u> (3, 4)

Bob: Mmm, I think I'd rather just go there with a tour, or on second thoughts, just stay here!

Liz: Shall I show you the net in action? Then you could think about it too and we could talk to each other!

Bob: <u>That'll be the day! You can't persuade me that easily!</u> (5)

Liz: Look, we'll go into a travel group called Rec Travel Asia – the Rec part tells us it's recreational and the other words are obvious. We'll see the sort of questions that have been posted here. Right... <u>Here's one: "Will be arriving in New Delhi, India on Saturday. Does anyone know if it's possible to cash travellers cheques at the airport</u> (6) ?" Now let's see if anybody's replied to that...

Bob: *Here's an answer* (6), isn't it? Below that little square...

Liz: Let me see, yes "<u>You can change money at the airport in Delhi – last time I arrived near 2 a.m. I had no real problem but as you're arriving on Saturday why not try older Delhi? There is more life there</u> (6)." See?

EXAM EXERCISE 2	1 C 5 C
	2 B 6 A
ANSWERS	3 C 7 B
	4 A

TAPESCRIPT

Max: I'm here at a Swan Rescue Centre with its Director John Walker. John, these swans really are beautiful white birds aren't they, with their lovely long necks and graceful movements?

John: Yes, indeed, and <u>the limited number of British rivers that have them</u> (1) are very lucky indeed, but at this time of year they have big problems.

Max: Well, tell me why your Centre – which is really a hospital isn't it – is necessary for these beautiful creatures.

John: It's very sad, but although you would think that there is nothing nicer to do in this summer weather than spend a happy afternoon down by the river, here we are only <u>one month into the fishing season and hundreds of water birds have already been injured.</u>(7)

Max: So, what is it that causes so much harm to them?

John: I can show you here in this box – <u>this is the sort of thing we find inside them, these hooks, weights, fishing wire and pieces of netting.</u> (2)

Max: We really are talking about large numbers, are we?

John: Well, we estimate that <u>at least 1100 swans die each year because of this dangerous rubbish left on the river banks – and probably more than that</u> (3,7) because smaller birds get stuck in the bushes and so on, so we don't ever find them. I would say about three quarters of all our swans' injuries are fishing-related.

Max: What is it that's happening here?

John: There you're looking at some baby swans, who are very sick and only have a 50% chance of living – they've all had operations to remove hooks from their throats – in fact <u>we can sometimes expect to be doing half a dozen operations like this a day</u> (4). And that costs a lot of money of course.

Max: Well now <u>there is a local, which means cheap rate, Helpline telephone number</u> (5), isn't there, <u>0980 564979</u> (6), which people can ring if they find any dangerous riverbanks or lakesides to report, or if they would like to offer help in any way.

John: Yes, we would urge members of the public and all <u>the many careful fishermen – and most of them are careful</u> (7) – to get in touch with any information they have.

Exam tip

The answers come in order while you're listening – though there may be extra clues elsewhere in the text to help you answer a particular question. So a calm and confident approach will help you organise your mind and thoughts.

6 Listening Trial Paper

Hello. I'm going to give you the instructions for this test. I'll introduce each part of the test and give you time to look at the questions. At the start of each piece you'll hear this sound:

tone

TAPESCRIPT

You'll hear each piece twice. Remember, while you're listening, write your answers in your book. You'll have time at the end of the test to copy your answers onto the separate answer sheet. The tape will now be stopped. Please ask any questions now, because you must not speak during the test.

PAUSE 5 seconds

Now look at Part 1. You'll hear people talking in eight different situations. For questions 1 to 8, choose the best answer, A, B or C.

PART 1

1 Two friends are exchanging travellers' stories.
  Why was the storyteller happy?

A His car was mended.
B The part was replaced.
C The mechanic did the job free.

PAUSE 5 seconds • tone

* You had a problem on your last holiday, didn't you? Something about needing a spare part, wasn't it?
* Not exactly. What happened was this: we broke down in the middle of nowhere in the South of France. A mechanic came from a village about 30 kilometres away, loaded the car onto his truck, drove us to the village and <u>got the car going</u> – they don't just replace parts over there, <u>they actually mend things</u>. I offered him my insurance vouchers in payment – I wasn't even sure he'd heard of the company but he took one look and accepted them without a problem. We only lost half a day. Insurance is really worth it.

PAUSE 2 seconds • tone • Repeat Question 1 • PAUSE 2 seconds

2 Listen to this account of a frightening experience.
  What happened to the speaker?

A He fell asleep.
B He hit something violently.
C He nearly fell off the Severn Bridge.

PAUSE 5 seconds • tone

I was looking forward to getting home. The past 48 hours had been extremely hard but for once the traffic flow was smooth and I felt in good shape as I drove onto the motorway, though I didn't much care for the thought of another 225 miles to go. By 4 p.m. I was safely across the Severn Bridge. If I'd felt tired at this point, I would have taken a break but I felt fine and was aware only of how terribly dull the drive was, so I pressed on without stopping. Suddenly <u>I was woken</u> by a violent shaking and I was instantly aware that <u>I had dropped off</u> and I was now travelling headlong towards a drop into who knows where.

PAUSE 2 seconds • tone • Repeat Question 2 • PAUSE 2 seconds

3 Listen to these two people discussing the invented language, Esperanto.
  What do we learn about Esperanto?

A It is quite like Polish.
B It was intended to bring peace.
C We don't know why it was created.

PAUSE 5 seconds • tone

- I learnt it in a fifth of the time it took me to learn German. When I started learning it, I didn't find it nearly as difficult as everyone said.
- But what use will it be? You already speak other languages, and Esperanto is not anyone's mother tongue – it's made up after all!
- Listen, do you know why it was made up?
- No – no-one does, I don't suppose.
- It was a Polish Jew who invented it – he lived about 100 years ago.
- He must be old!
- He's dead now, silly, but he was a very sensitive little boy, and <u>saw how people from different nationalities hated each other</u> in his home town. He thought it was partly becasue they couldn't understand each other's language and they didn't like Polish enough to learn it, so <u>he thought that a universal second language would help</u>.

PAUSE 2 seconds • tone • Repeat Question 3 • PAUSE 2 seconds

4 You will hear an Indian woman remembering part of her wedding celebrations.
What is this part of the ceremony for?

A to allow the bride's parents to stop quarrelling
B to stop the bride working too hard before the wedding
C to prepare the house and people for the wedding

PAUSE 5 seconds • tone

Everyone takes off their shoes and sits on the floor as the priest conducts the ceremony. It can last two hours or more. Traditional songs are sung about the wedding to be. <u>This ceremony is a way of bringing the gods into the house for the wedding</u> – there are offerings of all kinds of food and drink to satisfy them. The bride is painted with an orange liquid, to make her skin look bright, with a complicated design on her hands. According to tradition she doesn't work after the wedding until the orange disappears. <u>The bride's parents call for everyone in the house to make up their quarrels and arguments</u>. The women drive away evil spirits from the bride using leaves to sprinkle holy water to the four corners of the room.

PAUSE 2 seconds • tone • Repeat Question 4 • PAUSE 2 seconds

5 You will hear someone giving you instructions about something.
What is the speaker explaining how to do?

A back exercises
B life-saving
C horse riding

PAUSE 5 seconds • tone

<u>On your hands and knees, keep your arms and legs still and bend your head downwards, then curve your back to hollow it while you raise your head up.</u> That's it – very good. <u>This time, on your hands and knees again, bend one knee forward as you bend your head down so your forehead and knee touch. Stretch your leg out straight behind you and lift your head so your back curves slightly.</u> Be careful here, we don't want any injuries. Good, you're getting the hang of it! Now remember, after any exercising, sitting, lifting, gardening, riding etc., always <u>extend your back to regain the natural position.</u>

PAUSE 2 seconds • tone • Repeat Question 5 • PAUSE 2 seconds

6 You will hear a conversation between a waiter and a customer in a restaurant.
In which part of the restaurant are the customers going to have their meal?

A in a no-smoking area
B in a smoking area
C they'll decide when the brother arrives

PAUSE 5 seconds • tone

- Good evening Madam. Table for three, is it?
- Well actually there will be five of us, but the others haven't arrived yet, but they'll be here very shortly I'm sure.
- Certainly, Madam. Did you book or ....?
- Yes – in fact I rang yesterday and booked for four people – the name's Gunn...
- Ah, yes, here we are, Miss Gunn. Smoking or non-smoking?
- My brother said he was giving up but <u>I'm not convinced that he has</u>, and he's one of the people who haven't come yet.
- <u>Better safe than sorry</u> perhaps Madam? There's a table for five over here. I'll bring the menus to you there so you can think about it for a while, while you wait.
- Thank you. <u>I hope this polluted air's all right with the rest of you</u>. You'll have to blame my brother if not!

PAUSE 2 seconds • tone • Repeat Question 6 • PAUSE 2 seconds

7 You are in a Tourist Information Office. You hear an Assistant talking on the telephone. What did the caller telephone to find out about?

A restaurants
B nightclubs
C some telephone numbers

PAUSE 5 seconds • tone

Yes, if you just hold on a moment, I'll have a look... there are a couple of local ones – one in the High Street and one in the next town, Dubton. Do you know Dubton? Oh, it's not far and there are good buses. Well, the one here's the Nightjar and the one in Dubton's called Step Out, I think it is... <u>No other nightclubs</u> as far as I can see...What was that?...Oh, let me just check that for you. <u>Minimum age 18 for both</u>. Food? Snacks only it says, <u>so for a full meal you'd need a proper restaurant</u>... Oh, there's a good choice in Dubton... Entry fee? Can't tell you that – you'll have to ring. The Nightjar's number is 385923 and Step Out is 385717...Right, bye.

PAUSE 2 seconds • tone • Repeat Question 7 • PAUSE 2 seconds

8 You will hear a conversation between two young people playing a game. What happens to Linda?

A She wins the game.
B She laughs so much she can't finish.
C She loses the game.

PAUSE 5 seconds • tone

- <u>What you have to do is avoid saying Yes or No. If you say either of these, then you lose. OK?</u>
- I'll just stay quiet then!
- No you've got to answer the questions you're asked. Right, shall we start?
- Go on then, fire away...
- Where do you live?
- You know where I live!
- Is it nice there?
- It's all right.
- Do you have a boyfriend?
- I might – in fact I have.
- Do you like him?
- Course I like him – quite a lot actually...
- So you're thinking of getting married then?
- Shouldn't think so...
- Are you sure?

- <u>Yes</u> –
- Woops!

PAUSE 2 seconds • tone • Repeat Question 8 • PAUSE 2 seconds

That's the end of Part 1.

PART 2

Now turn to Part 2. You will hear a young woman, Julie, describing to a local journalist a car accident she had recently. For questions 9 - 18, fill in the information asked for by the news reporter. You'll need to write a word or a short phrase in each box. You now have forty-five seconds in which to look at Part 2

PAUSE 45 seconds • tone

Last <u>Wednesday</u> (9) I had just dropped my child off at school and was minding my own business in my <u>new blue sports car</u> (10), going about 30 miles an hour, on the left of course, when I came to a bend in the road curving off to my right, yeah? I was thinking about my little girl, and hoping she would enjoy her day – she was going to have a Maths test actually that morning and she felt quite nervous. Anyway, as I approached this bend there was <u>this small red car parked on the other side</u> (11), with its hazard lights flashing. Then suddenly a large white car – a Rolls Royce – came from nowhere towards me, breaking the speed limit I'm sure. He overtook the red car, came into my lane and I realised there was no way of avoiding him – I had no time to swerve out of his way: we hit each other head-on. Feeling rather shaken, I checked I could feel everything, and luckily only felt sore where the seatbelt had been, so I took it off and crossed the road. The other driver immediately said <u>how sorry he was</u> (13). <u>He had noticed the parked car, he said, but not in time</u> (12) then couldn't stop quickly enough – he hadn't realised <u>how fast he was going</u> (13). He asked me if I was all right. Then someone I recognised happened to drive past – it was a woman I'd met for the first time some weeks ago at a party and found we got on rather well. I've been meaning to ring her in fact. This was our first meeting since then and I waved to her. She stopped and smiled. I told her what had happened and <u>she very readily gave me a lift to my husband's office</u> (14), some 3 miles away. She was going more or less in that direction herself, so it wasn't too much out of her way. His colleagues made tea and rang the police, who asked me to return to the scene of the accident. There I found both the police and an ambulance waiting for me – I don't know who rang the ambulance, but they left when they saw no-one was hurt. <u>The police interviewed the drivers involved and analysed our breath, but we weren't drunk</u> (15) – (it was 9.15 a.m. after all!) The other driver was giving the Rolls Royce a final test drive after a service – <u>his customer was waiting to take it home</u> (16), so imagine how he felt at the news! I believe he owns a bank or something! Anyway, because <u>this other guy is a mechanic, the garage he works for</u> (17) offered to remove the vehicles from the road. <u>It could all have been so much worse – so I do feel very lucky</u> (18).

PAUSE 10 seconds • tone

Now you'll hear Part 2 again.

Repeat Part 2 • PAUSE 5 seconds

That's the end of Part 2.

Now turn to Part 3. You will hear five people reading out short articles from a newspaper. For Questions 19 - 23, choose from the list A - F which statement is true in which story. Use the letters only once. Remember that there is one extra statement which you do not need to use. You now have thirty seconds to look through Part 3.

PAUSE 30 seconds • tone

Nearly 300 staff will have to look for new jobs when the Opera House <u>closes for redevelopment next year</u>, it was announced yesterday. Announcing its plans for the two seasons that the house <u>will be closed after July this year</u>, they said the company would perform at several other theatres and go on tour in Britain and internationally. All being well, <u>audiences will be able to return to the Opera in the new building in a year's time</u>. The General Director, when interviewed about the situation, very much regretted that he could not keep all his staff during the time the Opera was closed.

PAUSE 2 seconds

The company, Flyaway Airways, agreed with their critics last week that their passengers no longer trusted them, and that <u>this was the end of the road</u>. It was set up in 1994, with 170 staff, and operated out of all the major airports in Britain. Earlier this month 39 passengers refused to board a Flyaway plane after they saw smoke coming from the aircraft. Last weekend 284 passengers had refused to board the same plane after a series of problems ended with the pilot slamming on the brakes as the plane reached top speed before take-off. <u>Customers who have already bought tickets with this airline will now be offered flights with another airline.</u>

PAUSE 2 seconds

Youngsters from the town of Middleton between the ages of 9 and 21 <u>will soon have a place to go</u> if they need any information or advice on matters like careers, health or personal matters. <u>The Advice Discovery Room, as it is to be called, will be organised by the youngsters themselves.</u> Five 14-year-old girls are behind the project and they have raised £500. <u>They intend</u> to offer anyone, both youth club members and young people from the general public, a friendly ear and a word of advice. The money will also go towards the boxes of information that they have collected together.

PAUSE 2 seconds

Long-haired Tim Dray from Chadborough saved an old people's home from closing. <u>Instead of going to his own hairdresser</u> yesterday morning, he waited for opening time in his local pub. There, <u>a friend was waiting for him with a pair of scissors</u>. A large number of people watched and gave money. "<u>It's the first time I've been bald</u>" he said afterwards, "<u>it's a bit cold</u> but it's worth it!" His action made over £500 and a representative of the Home said they were delighted to be able to carry on. Tim has done other mad things to make money. He was once on TV with a small biting animal down his trousers to help sick children. He closed the day by joining fishing friends on the nearby river, who gave another £72 towards the event.

PAUSE 2 seconds

Workers are greatly needed for an afterschool activity group <u>who fear having to close their doors for the last time</u>. The Youth Group, called the Eagles, have been going nationally for 10 years. They provide activities for young people aged between five and ten, like games, and arts and crafts. But <u>unless helpers aged 18 or over come forward, the service will be lost.</u> Spokeswoman Harriet Trim said: "We are in a desperate state. <u>If we don't find volunteers quickly, that will be that for us.</u>" The group meets once a week for around 90 minutes during school terms and has been extremely popular.

PAUSE 10 seconds • tone

Now you'll hear Part 3 again.

Repeat Part 3 • PAUSE 5 seconds

That's the end of Part 3.

PART 4

Now turn to Part 4. You will hear a conversation between Mrs Nelson and a visitor to her house. You will also hear Diana and Mr Nelson. For questions 24 - 30, decide which of the choices A, B, or C is the correct answer. You now have 30 seconds to look through Part 4.

PAUSE 30 seconds • tone

Mrs N: Hello – you must be Annie.

Annie: Hello. Mrs Nelson? (28)

Mrs N: <u>Yes, welcome</u> (23) – it's lovely <u>to meet you at last</u>... (24) How was your journey? I wonder how you like the tunnel under the sea?

Annie: Oh, it wasn't too bad – but the bus rocked a bit on the train. I slept most of the way though – better than the ferry any day. And it's always exciting <u>going to a new country</u> (24).

Mrs N: Well come in and put your bags down. That's it – now come through and I'll introduce you. <u>Come in from the garden</u> (29) you two, Annie's arrived – oh, look at all that mud! Take your boots off please – <u>this is little Ben and Andrew</u>... (25) (28)

Annie: Hello. They are very alike aren't they?

Mrs N: Yes, some people still can't tell them apart, so they prefer to dress differently – I'll show you where they keep everything when you're settled in. They're learning to cook at school, and there's the eldest of our three, <u>Diana</u>, over there – <u>she'll give you lots of help with the little ones I'm sure</u> (26) – Diana!

Diana: Hi! (28)

Annie: Hello.

Diana: What have you got there? Goodness, looks like a violin! Mmm, it's the guitar I want to learn.

Mrs N: Yesterday Ben and Andrew <u>made an apple pie for you, but they left it out by mistake on the work surface in the kitchen</u> (27) and the cat thought it was lovely...

(Annie laughs)

Mr N: Hello, you must be Annie. <u>I'm Henry Nelson</u> (28).

Annie: Oh, good afternoon Mr Nelson. It's a beautiful <u>house you have</u> (29) – I love the design.

Mr N: Attractive isn't it? Glad you like it. Shown you your room and everything, have they? <u>Oh, look at that. Will you give us a little concert tonight? I'd love to hear you play</u> (30).

Annie: I'm a bit out of practice I'm afraid...

Mrs N: Well, another day, perhaps. You know, my husband and I are both delighted that you're here because as I wrote to you, we're both rather busy with the business at present . Now, is there anything you want to ask me about before I take you upstairs and show you round? I can tell you about the area if you like – it's quite a nice town this, with lots to do on your days off and that sort of thing, and there are some people your age I want you to meet – in your spare time that is!

Annie: Oh, that sounds nice – it will be good for my English. I'd also like to know about the buses, and I wondered if there were any courses I could go on – I'd really like to take up something new... the trumpet maybe!

PAUSE 10 seconds • tone

Now you'll hear Part 4 again

Repeat Part 4 • PAUSE 5 seconds

That's the end of Part 4. There'll now be a pause of five minutes for you to copy your answers onto the separate answer sheet.

[**Note**. *The rest of this tapescript is not on the tape that goes with this book, but we have printed it here so that you will know what to expect in the exam.*]

I'll remind you when there is one minute left, so that you're sure to finish in time.

PAUSE 4 minutes

You have one more minute left.

PAUSE 1 minute

That's the end of the test. Please stop now. Your supervisor will now collect all the question papers and answer sheet. Goodbye.

Part 1
1 A
2 A
3 B
4 C
5 A
6 B
7 B
8 C

Part 2
9 Wednesday
10 blue, sports
11 parked on other / right-hand side
12 saw car too late
13 driving too fast / to blame
14 her husband's office
15 the drivers' breath (for alcohol)
16 (waiting) at the garage
17 a garage
18 it wasn't very serious

Part 3
19 E
20 C
21 D
22 B
23 A

Part 4
24 A
25 A
26 B
27 C
28 C
29 B
30 C

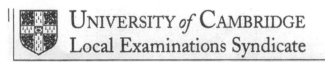

UNIVERSITY *of* CAMBRIDGE
Local Examinations Syndicate

SAMPLE

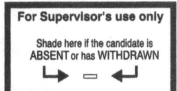
Examination Details	9999/04	99/D99

Examination Title First Certificate in English

Centre/Candidate No. AA999/9999

Candidate Name A.N. EXAMPLE

• Sign here if the details above are correct

X

• Tell the Supervisor now if the details above
  are not correct

Candidate Answer Sheet: FCE Paper 4 Listening

Mark test version below

A	B	C	D	E

Use a pencil

For **Parts 1** and **3**:
Mark ONE letter for
each question.

For example, if you
think **B** is the right
answer to the
question, mark your
answer sheet like this:

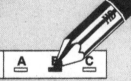

0	A	B	C

For **Parts 2** and **4**:
Write your answers in
the spaces next to the
numbers like this:

0	*example*

Part 1

1	A	B	C
2	A	B	C
3	A	B	C
4	A	B	C
5	A	B	C
6	A	B	C
7	A	B	C
8	A	B	C

Part 3

19	A	B	C	D	E	F
20	A	B	C	D	E	F
21	A	B	C	D	E	F
22	A	B	C	D	E	F
23	A	B	C	D	E	F

Part 2

	Do not write here
9	9
10	10
11	11
12	12
13	13
14	14
15	15
16	16
17	17
18	18

Part 4

	Do not write here
24	24
25	25
26	26
27	27
28	28
29	29
30	30

FCE-4

DP263/53